When Hope Whispers

When Hope Whispers

Zoleka Mandela

First published by Jacana Media (Pty) Ltd in 2013

10 Orange Street
Sunnyside
Auckland Park 2092
South Africa
+2711 628 3200
www.jacana.co.za

ISBN 978-1-4314-0904-4

Cover design by publicide
Set in Sabon 11/16pt
Printed by Ultra Litho (Pty) Ltd, Johannesburg
Job no. 002104

See a complete list of Jacana titles at www.jacana.co.za

To Zenani, Zwelami, Zenawe
And my unborn child ...

Acknowledgements

With Love and Gratitude

I INITIALLY BEGAN WRITING MY book in January of this year, just five months before I would sign a book deal as a first-time author with the intention of being published by Jacana Media. Three months after signing on the dotted line, my manuscript, which I had been working on for a period of nine months at that time, officially went into production – that was in September of the very the same year. It wasn't so much the eventuality that my autobiography would be rightfully subjected to public scrutiny that I found the most difficult, the challenge I was faced with was having to relive my most gruelling experiences, for lack of a better word, which I have taken a risk in sharing with you all. What I had initially intended on writing about – my journey with breast cancer – is not what eventually emerged in my book. Particularly, the passing of my late daughter and late son (Zenani and Zenawe), my decade-long addiction to cocaine and alcohol and sharing the difficulty I still have in not disclosing the details of my sexual abuse and undiagnosed sex addiction to a much larger extent.

If I didn't write this book, then my tears that turned its pages did.

These past few months of having to reflect on very personal and intimate issues in my life, which I am no longer entirely ashamed about and which I have come to accept as life's many brutal lessons, I strongly believe have made me a much stronger person – the person that I am today. I take pride in what I have written and it has been thoroughly and phenomenally rewarding.

To my fellow breast cancer survivors, survivors of sexual abuse, those struggling with addiction and to those who have lost their loved ones – it is my hope that if you are reading this book, in the end, the realisation of one of my many passions has been a successful one – having my life experiences save and change, even if it is just one person's life, for the positive. I am thankful for the lesson that I have learned: that I will have to change and use my life if I want to make a profound impact on my society and the world at large, no matter the risk.

This book wouldn't have been possible without the unwavering support structure I have been blessed to have. I cannot imagine how I would have made it this far without the unconditional love, support, understanding and patience I have received from everyone. In particular, my grandfather Nelson Rolihlahla Mandela, one of my closest friends and grandmother Nomzamo Winfred Madikizela Mandela, my grandmother Graça Machel, my confidant and maternal aunt Her Excellency, Ambassador Zenani Mandela, my son Zwelami Mandela, my brother Zondwa Mandela, my partner and manpower Thierry Bashala, and my sister-in-law Lindo Mandela. I know that I have also been blessed with two legendary angels watching over us and walking either side of me – my daughter and best friend, Zenani Mandela and my son, Zenawe Mandela. I would like to take this opportunity to thank each and every one of you for the profound impact you have had on my life and for the woman that I am today. Know that these words of your personal contribution to my life are written with you especially in my mind and heart and as I salute you all for being the foundation of my strength, the curve to my smile and the very warmth in my heart, I hope that I will one day make you proud if I haven't already done so.

To those who I call my second family, I am most thankful for the opportunity of being cared for by Dr Carol Ann Benn, my breast specialist surgeon and my oncologist, Dr Georgia Demetriou of the Breast Care Centre of Excellence in Netcare Milpark Hospital and the Wits Donald Gordon Medical Centre. An extended thank you goes to Dr Merwyn Jacobson, Sister Ann Hacking and Bernice List of the Vitalab In Vitro Fertility (IVF) Clinic. The medical staff at these places have offered amazing support without which I doubt my experience would have been as bearable or as memorable. I am grateful to have passed through your care.

To Houghton House Addiction Recovery Centre, my home away from home that treated me for my alcohol and drug addiction, thank you for providing me with a safe and supportive home in my time of complete desperation and self-loathing. I also want to thank you for saving my life; affording me the chance to at least give myself the best gift

I could in staying clean and sober. Thank you once again for introducing me to all the friends in recovery I have met at Houghton House, and the Narcotics Anonymous and Alcoholics Anonymous Fellowships.

To Zodwa Zwane, Thatohatsi Motsoane and Ms Zintle Mjali, I thank the three of you for the abundance of tears, laughter and love we have shared together in the months and years we have known one another. I may not have known you for a lifetime, but it sure feels like I have loved you that long.

To Timothy Maurice Webster, who I always refer to as my personal guru, I thank you for teaching me how to channel my emotional energy into my writing and for the encouragement and support you've always given me from the very first time I told you that I was ready to write a book. Thank you for always being such a source of inspiration and for the introduction you facilitated with Jacana Media. When I first met my publisher, Thabiso Mahlape, she had wanted to have me sign the contract not knowing who I was but because she had already developed a respect, common passion and interest for what I had originally envisaged for my book. I thank her for allowing me to be an even better writer but more profusely for believing in me when I doubted myself. I thank my editor, Nicola Menne, for turning my manuscript into something one would want to read. To my publicist, Samantha Gibb, and the rest of the Jacana Media team who have done such a remarkably outstanding job in the organisation, marketing and publishing of my book, *When Hope Whispers*, your dedication and effort remain unforgettable. A heartfelt thank you to Debbie Yezbek who captured the amazing image used for my book and Iko Mash for the beautiful make-up for the cover.

It would be such an injustice not to refer to the remainder

of my close friends and family and that also goes for all of my son's teachers, friends and family from Saint Stithians College who have been greatly supportive. A big thank you goes to all my friends on Facebook, Twitter, WhatsApp and BBM for never judging me and continuing to inspire me through all your positive feedback and comments.

Lastly; to my furry sons Benzeey and Thizo, the only two Jack Russell terriers who have consumed a place in my heart ... It's funny, they don't believe me when I say it, but you've helped me heal too!

Foreword

THE LAST THREE YEARS FROM 2010, 2011, 2012 including part of 2013 have been very difficult years for my family. One of the most affected of my twenty-something grandchildren is Zoleka Mandela, the eldest of Zindzi's children.

It is rare to write a foreword for your grandchild, but the circumstances that led to this foreword are of a book born out of so much pain that it obscures my own painful experiences, which are in my publication of a prison journal titled *491 Days* which was never conceived for publication.

As a grandmother, I have been with Zoleka throughout the darkest days of her life together with the family that reached out to her and embraced her with unconditional love. I will not refer to any of the tragic incidents in her life as this is her own story to tell. All I'll try to do is share with the future readers Zoleka's amazing strength, which we observed as she battled to rise above her personal tragedy, and rather telescope the bigger picture so as to inspire millions of women out there, to give them hope and tell them that breast cancer today is no longer a death sentence. She is a brave survivor of the greatest test in any woman's life because of her strength of character and resolve.

But this resolve was not arrived at easily. I remember the first call I received from her after she had been to see a doctor for the first time. At this stage I would like to caution all young women about the importance of checking the credentials of the doctor. Without my knowledge, Zoleka had been nursing a lump that had mutated on her left breast until it grew bigger and bigger. She confided in her aunt Princess Zenani Dlamini, now her Excellency Ambassador to Argentina.

Her aunt advised her to rush to a doctor who neglected to inform her of her condition. She phoned me very distraught. A few days later the same doctor, who still hadn't informed my granddaughter of her condition, phoned her to refer her to another doctor. We then decided against this referral and took her to a breast cancer specialist, Dr Carol Ann Benn at the Breast Care Centre of Excellence of the Netcare Milpark Hospital as suggested by her aunt Princess Zenani Dlamini. We owe Dr Benn and Dr Demetriou, Zoleka's oncologist, a debt of gratitude not easy to translate into words. They have both been with Zoleka throughout this hurtful journey to this day.

To our horror as a family, Zoleka, upon receiving her diagnosis and for three months after this, said she did not want treatment. For two months I was treated for acute insomnia. The last time I felt that way was during my own ordeal of eighteen months in solitary confinement. Together with the family, I watched her dying each day. I knew each one of us, as family, prayed silently for her to change her mind. In fact, we suffered silently just like her. In my case, I was afraid to persuade her because I was terrified of her repeating that she was ready to die. To my surprise, I realised she was actually stronger than all of us. I had never heard of anyone on death row saying they were prepared to die.

During this period, we visited her doctor, who lectured her each time, persuading her that her type of cancer was a "very lazy" cancer, meaning that it was developing very slowly. Sadly none of this talk persuaded her. Instead she became withdrawn and made it difficult for us to even raise the subject.

One day, after three months, when we had gone for the usual consultations, she made a call to Dr Benn to inform her that she was now ready for treatment. I had observed that in the three months she became even more attached to her son, my great-grandson, who was just about 9 years old. I was to learn much later that she feared a life of an invalid who was in and out of hospital, a protracted death that would render her dependent on someone. Ultimately though, it dawned on her that her young son would watch her going through all that and she couldn't bear the thought.

Then the journey towards her healing began. I found it very difficult to watch her going through that chemotherapy treatment, as with all her tragedies. I cannot emphasise enough the importance of the moral support of the family.

As a grandmother I wished I could take the pain on her behalf! The endless drawing of blood from her veins, the drips, her reaction, the side effects, and so on. And yet this was the time Zoleka showed her amazing strength, which grew every day. Her decision to live was a battle half won.

Her aunt Princess Zenani called every week from Argentina, each call coincided with the exact time of her treatment. The day she completed her treatment was like the day she was born.

Zoleka's rebirth produced a brand new personality, an even more loving and caring mother who has already given numerous talks on breast cancer. Her resolve to help millions of women out there is very touching. She is leading a United Nations campaign on road safety and the dangers of drunken driving. Through the Zenani Mandela Campaign, she is as totally committed to helping reduce the deaths on the roads as she is about promoting awareness of breast cancer.

She has become a health fanatic. I know that she now runs five kilometres every Saturday morning and eats a very healthy diet. From the days of chemotherapy when she could barely eat, sometimes it is a great pleasure to watch the brand new Zoleka at play. She treats each day as a life time and is extremely concerned about the general health of her family.

I know Zoleka will remain as she is for the rest of her life. My family and I are as excited as the general public who have listened to her interviews and have given awesome reviews and great words of encouragement. I join that public in thanking Zoleka for being an epitome of courage, strength, commitment and dedication to the cause of helping millions and millions of women out there.

GrandMa Zanyiwe Winnie Nobandla Mandela!

PART I

I learned that courage is not the absence of fear, but the triumph over it. The brave man is not he who does not feel afraid, but he who conquers that fear.

~ Nelson Rolihlahla Mandela

Chapter 1

BY THE TIME I WAS BORN, ON 9 April 1980, my mother knew how to strip and assemble an AK-47 in exactly thirty-eight seconds. She was twenty years old, trained in guerilla warfare and already a full-fledged member of Umkhonto we Sizwe.

I was born to Zindziswa Nobutho Mandela and Oupa Johannes Mafanyana Seakamela at Marymount Maternity Home in Kensington, Johannesburg. My mother, Zindzi, is the second daughter of Nelson Rolihlahla Mandela and Nomzamo Winfred Madikizela-Mandela. My grandfather, Nelson Mandela, was one of the founding members of Umkhonto we Sizwe when it formed in 1961, at a time when the African National Congress was banned under apartheid. By the late 1970s my grandmother, Nomzamo, known to others as Winnie, was using my father to pose as her driver while she trained him to recruit MK comrades. My father would hide and transport military weapons as he moved between Swaziland, Botswana and Lesotho.

To say I was born in the thick of it is an understatement.

Before I was a year old, my grandmother had already smuggled me into Robben Island on her back. She says that at the time it was the only gift she could give my grandfather, who by then had not seen a baby for many years. As it was, the law of the country stipulated that only one child could visit at a time from each family, and visiting children had to be sixteen years and older. My mother had managed to visit her father because she'd been able to pass herself off as a sixteen-year-old when she was fourteen.

With my grandfather's political career – in fact, his life – unquestionably committed to an anti-apartheid South Africa, he had never been able to be the father he wanted to be for his own children. His legacy lived on in my mother, who was politically active in her own right.

When I was a toddler, my mother sent me to Swaziland for three years, where I lived with her older sister, my aunt Princess Zenani, my uncle, Prince Thumbumuzi Dlamini, and my cousins. My earliest memory is from that time in Mbabane: I remember sitting on the floor in my aunt and uncle's lounge, my back against the couch. My aunt was sitting on the floor to my right, her legs straight out and crossed at the ankles, and we were watching television. As the news came on she said, "It is your birthday today. You are four years old!" I remember wondering where my mother was and why she wasn't with me.

When I think of my mother in those early years, I don't know why I remember the things I do: the times she would braid my hair as I sat between her legs, and how she parted it in the middle and plaited the one side as I rested my head on the warmth of her inner thigh; how she would put me to sleep before she left me and how pained I so often was waking up to the realisation that she was gone.

My heart aches now, thinking of this, as I remember my own daughter, Zenani, between the ages of four and five, and how she used to cry each time I left her. Especially as I know that I didn't have to leave.

My memories are elusive, like whispers, but some details of my early years come back to me: I remember that back in those days, my aunt drove a metallic blue Honda with an all-black interior. My upbringing in Swaziland resonates with nostalgic tunes, such as Gregory Abbott's "Shake You Down", Teddy Pendergrass's "In My Time," The Jacksons' "Can You Feel It", Billy Ocean's "Get Outta My Dreams, Get Into My Car" and "We Are the World" by USA For Africa.

I remember that even at that young age I, like my cousins, always had black synthetic braids plaited into my hair – the older we got the more beads we placed on our braided fringes. I attended two nursery schools in Swaziland but I can't recall anything more than the walk my cousin and I would take in the mornings with our nanny: there was tall grass alongside the path, and the morning dew would some days leave wet traces on our pants. I remember how in the mornings we children had Maltabella for breakfast, but my aunt would opt for black tea and toast. She'd bite off a piece of toast, chew it a few times and then sip her tea before swallowing the toast. I always admired how eloquently she did that.

I remember how my cousins and I would get back from school first, and how excited I always was for my aunt and uncle to arrive home. The highlight of my day was seeing them, but perhaps that was because of the physical abuse my cousins and I sustained at the hands of our nanny. I soiled my bunk bed one morning and I recall how petrified I was coming home. When we were being punished, my cousins and I were instructed to go outside into the yard and pick a stick, which we then had to put in a tub to soak. Naked, we'd all lie next to one another on a bed awaiting a lashing by our nanny, who would decide whether she would start from the youngest or the oldest child. I wasn't allowed any water in the evenings due to my bed wetting, but when I was thirsty I'd drink water from the bathroom tap. If our nanny found me doing that, she'd knock my head against it, or use her knuckles on my skull. My cousins and I were always being struck with belts, hangers and cords.

Chapter 2

IN 1985, WHEN MY AUNT, MY uncle and my cousins moved to Boston, Massachusetts, I was returned to my mother. She was by then living with my grandmother in Brandfort, in what was then the Orange Free State – my grandmother had been living there since 1977, when she'd been banished there by the government. It was a desolate area with a few cattle, barns and chicken coops, and we lived in a dusty township outside a stark Afrikaner town. My brother, Zondwa, had been born in 1983, but soon after I arrived in Brandfort, my mother left for Johannesburg, taking my brother with her.

In Brandfort I developed a very close bond with a girl called Naledi, whose house was situated next to ours. Back then there were no fancy gates or fences to separate the houses; neither were there toilets, baths or showers in the houses, and on some occasions Naledi and I would share a bath in a big steel tub on her family's stoep. I remember how Naledi and I were once playing at the front of a neighbour's house, and how quickly we ran when he stormed towards us with a pointed gun. I remember the smell of the toilets, which were more like long drops in those days, and how these were emptied once a week. My grandmother used to make atchar, which she sold to the neighbours in big, round yellow tubs with handles. I would sit in the kitchen watching her decanting the atchar. To this day I can eat an entire tub of atchar from a glass jar if I want to.

My grandmother and my mother were very busy with service-orientated projects. As there was no other clinic in the township, my grandmother had, with the assistance of the Anglican Church, built a clinic in our yard, and two doctors would drive from Johannesburg to treat the patients. My mother worked for Operation Hunger and she passed on food supplies to my grandmother, who in turn gave them out to the community.

There was a lot of activity when I was at home in exile.

———•———

I wasn't in Brandfort for long, although my grandmother had been there for nine years, because in 1986 my family moved back to my grandparents' home, 8115 Vilakazi Street, Orlando West – in what is now the Nelson Mandela Museum. Once in Soweto, I started at a Montessori primary school because my grandmother preferred the child-focused Montessori method over more conventional types of schooling.

The school was situated on the outskirts of Johannesburg,

in Woodmead. We school children used to fill an entire minibus as we travelled back and forth between our school in the suburbs and our homes in Soweto, where our families were distributed across Orlando, Rockville, Diepkloof, Pimville and other areas. It was always the same driver who drove us. He sold us biltong sticks, and would alternate the order of drop-offs depending on who he had collected first: so sometimes those of us at school in Woodmead would be the last bunch to get dropped off at school, having spent what felt like hours in the taxi.

In our free time at the Montessori primary school we built forts in the woods in the school grounds, and I enjoyed cooking lessons and eating pomegranates. We loved playing with our teacher's brown dog, and I recall being so alarmed and sad one afternoon when a snake squirted its lethal venom into one of his eyes.

My first boyfriend taught me how to kiss and hold hands; I "dated" him for a year and a half from the tender age of nine. We used the same transport, and so we would save seats for each other if we didn't get to the taxi at the same time.

From that very young age I felt quite different from the other children, and I suppose in reality I was. I was obsessed with pregnant women, and my grandmother and mother were called into my school by my teacher after it was noted that I had been drawing images of pregnant women in my school book. Playing with my Barbie in my bedroom at home, I was always grabbing pieces of cloth or Barbie's clothing, rolling it up into a ball in my hand and putting it underneath whatever dress or top Barbie was dressed in to show that she was pregnant.

Our house at 8115 was extremely small: it consisted of one bedroom, a kitchen, one bathroom directly opposite the kitchen, a dining room and a sitting room. I can recall my grandmother, mother and my brother Zondwa and I all sleeping in that one bed.

We spent some of our time watching television in the lounge, but mostly we children could be found playing outside with the rest of the children in the neighbourhood – the same children who would later feature in Brenda Fassie's music video "Ag Shame, Lovey". My two girl cousins were visiting from the States at the time, and we narrowly missed the opportunity to be in the music video when it was decided that it would be inappropriate for us to participate. We already had our matching leotards, leg warmers and head bands, and I remember how disappointed I was not to be in Aunty Brenda's video.

Every day we had to be back home by five to have a bath, and I remember how the dust would literally cling to our bodies after a game of *morabaraba*, *bhati*, *black mampatile* or *mogusha*. Afterwards it felt like we'd been dipped into a human-sized Vaseline tub: you could always tell when we had washed because we left the house with extremely glossy skin.

In 1989 our house at 8115 was burned to the ground. On the day it happened, my brother Zondwa and I left school and, unusually, were taken to my grandmother's office instead of straight home. There, the parking lot was filled with journalists. We were ushered into her office and it was only then that we were told why we couldn't go home. I remember being most excited about the new clothes Zondwa and I would now have to get! While it was being rebuilt, we moved to the home of a family friend in Dube, just a few streets away from my father's family home, although we didn't stay there for very long.

We then stayed in a house in Diepkloof Extension Phase 2, and it was in this year that my brother Bambatha was born. This home was more spacious than our house at 8115. I had my own room, where I hung a school photo of my boyfriend, who used to pay me visits there. When I had mumps, I sat cooped up in my bedroom for hours, while everyone else played outside. As warm as the weather was, I was self-conscious enough to conceal the swelling of the lower part of my face and jaw with a scarf.

In many ways my life in those very early years was untainted and innocent. Some memories cause my heart to smile, despite the strained political times in which we were living.

Home, after all, was home.

There was even an advantage to having my Aunt Zenani and cousins living abroad: they always ensured that we had the best toys, clothing, magazines and music. The fact that it all came from America was such a big deal – especially to the other kids in the neighbourhood. When my cousins had returned to the States after visiting us in Diepkloof, I was often teased about my wonderful new possessions.

It was also in Diepkloof Extension that I developed a liking for BMX bicycles. I had one in blue, which I rode up and down the long street with a bunch of other kids – they could perform the most admirable tricks on them, which I couldn't. Quite the tomboy, I often played with my brother Zandwa and a son of one my grandmother's confidants, a former agent from the time of her banishment. In fact, in an open area just opposite my home I once accidentally cut myself with a wire, deep on the inside of my right thigh while we were trapping pigeons to eat – I was usually responsible for stealing spices from the house while the boys killed and removed the feathers from the bird before making a small fire to cook it on. In my own spare time, you would find me pulling apart yellow-and-black ladybirds when I found them mating *esgangeni* (the open area where we used to play) because it made me so sick to my stomach.

In our Diepkloof home I would join my grandmother, my mother and the comrades at the back of the house near our glossy blue Jacuzzi, where we'd sing freedom songs every evening. I got used to seeing the cadres hiding with their weapons in the house, because it was also what my grandmother called a "transit camp", which was then being used to recruit for Umkhonto we Sizwe. There was never one particular group of comrades, but an influx of new faces almost every day, with a few female comrades also thrown into the mix.

I am reminded of the lunches we shared with the cadres, and it felt like we were one big family. We would occupy the upstairs seating area of the Mike's Kitchen restaurant on St Andrews Road in Parktown. Sitting in the privacy of that space, there was always much drinking and laughing, and we always all ordered the same meal: the half-rib-and-prawn combo with French fries. The meal was good, but the love shared around that table was even better!

On one occasion my mother took me along with some of the comrades to fetch my grandmother from the airport. My grandmother describes how on this particular day – a day on which my mother had had a hand grenade in her possession – I spared her a life sentence. I am told that on the return trip, when the car in which we were travelling was surrounded by police, I boldly offered to conceal a hand grenade in my school bag – even at the age of nine I knew that my bag would be the last place the police would look. Thinking back, I remember how often my mother boastfully related this story, and how tired I became of hearing it. It always felt like something so important to her; in her eyes, it was something that I should have been extremely proud of.

My grandmother was arrested by the police yet again that day – this time for returning to Johannesburg while she was still banned to Brandfort, even though her home there had been burnt down too. Thinking back, I realise how often it happened, and how she resisted arrest every single time. In Diepkloof Extension I often saw the cadres being arrested themselves by the police, although I don't recall ever shedding a tear. I had grown very close to a cadre called Monde; but I didn't cry even when he was taken away, for it all to become just another incurable childhood memory.

"He was quite fond of you, darling, and I think you transferred your father figure emotions onto him," my grandmother told me later.

It seems I was already becoming used to loving, and losing.

—◦—

In Diepkloof we didn't have a swimming pool, and my brother Zondwa and I would have to ask permission from Dr Nthato Motlana to swim in his. Sure, we had a pool at the Montessori school – it was actually there that I was taught to swim – but it was always so exciting to have the opportunity to swim in a pool close to home. We often used to walk from 8115 to the public swimming pool in Orlando West. Almost as often, we would be crushed to discover that for whatever reason they had closed early.

In the late 1980s I was taken to visit my grandfather at

the Victor Verster Prison near Paarl in Cape Town. After being treated for TB in hospital, he had been transferred there from Pollsmoor Prison, having left Robben Island in 1982, and was staying in a private house. The government had made this move so they could soften him up and begin talks with the ANC in private.

For my part, I remember how breathtaking the elongated blue pool was there, and the beautiful table setting that was laid for lunch that afternoon, with two types of glasses, two types of knives and forks, cotton serviettes and a tablecloth large enough to cover the huge table. I don't remember the conversation we had, but I do recall that the house at Victor Verster was face brick, with a pastel-coloured lounge where we sat with my grandfather before and after lunch.

We all used to dress up to visit our grandfather in those days, and I remember all my cousins and me, along with our aunts, our mothers and our grandfather all sitting down to the most scrumptious food, including a fully glazed duck as the central attraction. There had never been any black wardens at the time of my grandfather's imprisonment, so none of us were shocked to have a white warden serving us, or a white chef cooking our meal.

Chapter 3

WHEN MY GRANDFATHER WAS released from prison in February 1990, I was almost ten years old. I know that I was too young to understand the significance of the day. Although I knew that we were celebrating our grandfather coming home, I couldn't have explained to you why we couldn't do so with just our family, in the comfort of our own home. There I am in the pictures taken on 11 February, but I couldn't relate to you how this defining day would change South Africa forever, and how it would bring ease to those affected so viciously by apartheid.

Sitting in a helicopter with him, my grandmother and my brother Zondwa, I looked through the window and down over Orlando Stadium and saw all those people looking back at us. As many, if not more, as I had seen looking at him the previous day as he delivered his first ever speech after his release at the City Hall in Cape Town.

But there were private matters to deal with at the same time as his very public release. Because of the damage to my grandfather's left lung, my grandmother was advised by the doctors to move him to a bigger house with more access to fresh air than the one they had shared at 8115. In the year following the fire we had moved back to Vilakazi Street, but about a year later, my grandmother, my grandfather, my mother, my two brothers and two of my male cousins moved into a bigger home over the mountain in Orlando West.

My first memory of that house is the eight o'clock bedtime curfew that was instilled by my grandfather. Even then he was making up his own bed and doing one hundred push-ups a day.

Although I didn't live with my father, I frequently visited his family home in Dube, which was not too far from my grandmother's house. My father had also done his fair share of relocating, and I spent time with him in the homes he owned in Eldorado Park and Pimville.

During the time he was in Eldorado Park, Ricardo's song "I love you, Daddy" was one of my favourites. Apart from the melody, I loved how Ricardo made me feel like he knew just how I felt about my own daddy. Sadly, that is my only positive memory of that home, which my recently married father shared with my new step-mother, who had been friends with my mother and my Aunt Zenani growing up. I remember seeing her standing on a chair hooking curtains to the curtain rail above the lounge window when I walked into the house. It wasn't too long afterwards that they had a spat during which I heard my step-mother ask my father to choose between her and me.

— My father took me home.

By the time they moved to Pimville in 1992, things had improved between us. Although my step-mother had me cooking, cleaning and babysitting my sisters and cousin at the age of twelve, I am at least grateful for the benefit of learning those skills. But I especially loved all the pairs of shoes she owned, and because she had such small feet, I knew it wouldn't be too long before I would be able to borrow them. It took some time, but I came to adore her: she was my daddy's wife and she became a mother to me. I remember laughing to myself when she asked my father why he hadn't hit me when I had deliberately sat on a swing in the park near their home instead of walking to church, which she'd instructed me to do.

My father often told me about how he used to take me everywhere with him when I was a baby in diapers, and that even at that age I was quite possessive over him. I refused to let any women dance with him at the parties we attended together, so he would make me stand on a table while he held my hands and he'd dance with me. He also told me how, when I was older, we would ride on his red motorbike all over Soweto. When I later told him I wanted a motorbike, he replied that I might as well buy a coffin to go with it because motorbikes are so dangerous – something he experienced first-hand when he was involved in an accident, though thankfully it only resulted in several very visible stitches to his arm.

My father was always mischievous: he started rumours of how he had gained possession of one of his favourite minibuses, and told stories about how in Soweto he'd once driven two cars at the same time because he needed to get them both to the same destination. On one New Year's Eve at my grandmother's home in Orlando West – what we call "Parliament" – while the family gathered to watch the firecrackers consume the night, I remember feeling the utmost excitement when my father took out his gun and allowed me to shoot in the air a few times. "Daddy Oupa", as everyone knows him, was one of those dads that everyone wished they had. The same goes for my mother.

In everyone's eyes, I had the coolest parents that no child would trade for the world.

I went to the Woodmead Montessori Primary School up until the end of 1990, and then refused to return because I felt that my teacher at the time hated me and that I was being treated unfairly. In 1991 I started at Sacred Heart College, repeating standard two because I'd failed it at the Montessori. I felt awkward at my new school, and I hated how I was always the tallest girl in the class – even more so because I seemed to be developing physically much quicker than all the other girls.

By 1992 my mother had married my step-father and had moved us to a home in Observatory near Bez Valley, east of Johannesburg, which was directly opposite my new school. My mother had had another baby – my brother Zwelabo – and my Aunt Zenani's two daughters and son, my cousins, had finally returned to South Africa from Boston. They moved in with us too.

Remembering my years at Sacred Heart I am taken back to the times when we'd attend socials at our school, or at nearby schools like Athlone Boys' and Athlone Girls' High.

Boys II Men had released "End of the road", and when the lights dimmed and that song came on you'd hope you were holding onto the guy you had a crush on and no one else. At school we wore tights under our yellow tunics because the boys used to stick mirrors on top of their shoes so they could see our underwear, or they'd wait until we were climbing up the stairs before finding an angle that would give them the best view.

Back then, my friends and I wrote to our pen pals, and my cousins and I innocently made pacts with each other that we had to keep: "You do not talk to him or even *look* at him, because I saw him first," or, "Don't look at him because I like him, even if he doesn't like me." Those were the days of waiting by the phone for "him" to call, and he always did. Letters were handwritten and followed strict guidelines: Name, Place, Time, Date, Reason and Song Dedication. This was followed by a squirt of perfume. I chose a deep red lipstick for leaving lip prints on my letters: "Sealed with a kiss 'cos a lick won't stick." I don't remember where I got that from but I loved it and made it mine.

At that young age, I was already quite insecure about my figure, although I was far from being overweight. The women on my father's side of the family have very large hips and buttocks, which I inherited – these, however, didn't faze me as much as my big lips and oversized forehead. I also remember hating how my legs looked in those little white socks we wore with our summer uniform. Most of the women in my family have my grandfather's thick legs, which he apparently got from his mother: if we're lucky enough to find a pair of boots that zip over our calves, you can still see our over-exaggerated trademark "cankles". I am reminded of someone once asking me how I was able to walk with ankles and legs that looked like they were swollen! At school, as I neared my teenage years, I always loved the long grey winter socks that covered my legs – I would wear them all the way above my knee so that there were only a few centimeters of flesh above the top of my socks and the bottom of my dark-grey winter skirt which, like the other girls, I wore rolled up at the waist.

I started dieting quite young, and working out on a white-and-black exercise machine I had in my bedroom. I think I must have been about fifteen when I started buying diet pills called Thinz and Redupon at a chemist in Yeoville.

My friends and I formed a girl group – we'd sing and dance, and spent most of our afternoons rehearsing for shows we held after school on the lawn at my Observatory home. On the odd occasion we would be requested to perform at other schools, and I remember my cousins and I having to audition in the gymnasium. In our tunics we gyrated to Wreckx-N-Effect's "Rump shaker", and we knew we had the part when the boys we were auditioning for started clapping even before our dance routine was over. They were all older than me and I had a crush on one of them for three long years. I'd never found the boys in my own age group attractive, and I was always keen on guys much older than me. By the time I got to high school everyone knew about my crush on the older boy – which I suppose was my fault because I never shied away from talking about my feelings for him.

"So, what does it feel like to kiss when you have braces on?" he once asked me, and it wasn't too long after his Matric finals that he mastered the art of kissing my fifteen-year-old self – with a mouth full of braces.

I hated those braces and wore them for two years before I had them removed, against the advice of the orthodontist. If I had known then what I know now, I would have kept them on for as long as I needed to. Even now I hate my teeth.

As the years past, we began to venture further away from our immediate neighbourhood. We started hanging out at Kine Centre, the Carlton Centre and the Carlton Hotel, which in those years were abuzz with teenagers and grown men.

———

I thought I was so grown up, but in reality I was very troubled.

From the time I was barely eight years old up to the age of fourteen, I had been sexually abused by some of the adults in my life who should have been looking after me. It is a story for another time and another platform, but the scars from these experiences have never truly healed. And they have everything to do with the hurt, defensive teenager I was becoming.

I had very low self-esteem and a deep fear of rejection, and I cultivated a thuggish, dark and hard image, when inside I was actually vulnerable and weak. My mother signed me up for a self-esteem class, which I didn't particularly enjoy. Instead, I traded my Barbies for pocket knives and knuckle dusters.

Chapter 4

ONE EVENING IN 1993, I FOUND myself on the floor, pleading with the devil to release my thirteen-year-old body.

My cousins and I had thrown a party at my Aunt Zenani's place in Walkerville – it was being held in the club house, which was at the end of an eight-door garage closest to the house. For what felt like hours, I faced the ceiling as I lay on the floor of the bar area, my hands at my sides as if I had been put on an invisible stretcher. No matter how hard I tried to twist myself out of the devil's grip, each time I opened my eyes I knew I hadn't moved an inch. It felt like when you're in a deep sleep, and you dream that you're awake, and no matter how much you try to move your hands and legs, or speak and shout, you are unable to move. You wake up and find yourself crying with helplessness.

I was in pure hell.

I was once told that this happens when your ancestors have come to visit you – although it was never explained to me why. There was only one reason I left the party that night, and it had nothing to do with my ancestors, and everything to do with the paranoia that had crept in after my first smoke of a marijuana joint. And so I attempted to hide for fear that everyone would think I couldn't handle my liquor and weed. I was wasted.

"Zoleka, don't mix alcohol and weed," I'd been warned when I'd asked for a few pulls. Of course, I should have been told not to drink or smoke weed *at all*, though I seldom listened to this kind of advice anyway. As I grew into my teenage years, my drinking and weed smoking together would often lead to violent outbursts, after which I would blackout. Even the traumatic experience of my first drink was not enough to stop me from drinking again – at nine years old I'd found a bottle of Martell VO brandy at home while I was playing with my grandmother's ex-agent's son. I'd finished it neat, and had to be rushed to Dr Motlana's home down the road.

By the time I was thirteen, I'd found that alcohol was the easiest and quickest way to overcome my unbearable shyness.

On the night of the party, the combination of the marijuana with the copious amounts I'd been drinking had me hiding on the other side of the bar counter so that I wouldn't be seen. I was too high to simply walk up the tiled stairs to a bedroom, where I would surely have felt safer with a door locked behind me. It was a while later that I realised I was being picked up by four guys I didn't know, who had found me passed out on the bar floor. The door leading to the bar was opposite the staircase leading to the upstairs bedrooms, and so I remember thinking when they picked me up – each holding my arms or legs – that they were taking me upstairs so that I could go to sleep. Instead, they turned towards the blue guest bathroom at the bottom of the staircase.

It turned out that the four guys had other plans.

I fought against them, but I was being pulled into the bathroom when a male friend happened to walk past. He insisted that I was his girlfriend and they let me go, but it seems they were only compelled to resist their urges because I "belonged" to him.

I was lucky.

As with my history of drinking alcohol, that would not be the last time I smoked marijuana. I hated the paranoia that came along with it but I could never decline the offer to light up, and eventually one too many "puff, puff, give" situations led to the point where I was rolling my own weed and smoking it in the comfort of my own bathroom. In our Observatory house, my tiny, maroon-tiled bathroom was past a closet area which I shared with my brothers; it had a little window which opened up to a view of the garden all the way from the gate to the front door. It was easy to smoke there: I would place my towel on the floor to seal the crack at the bottom of the bathroom door, and sit on the toilet with my head almost outside the window so that the smoke of my cigarettes or marijuana joint would escape the room – although it always clung to my breath, fingertips and clothing. From there, I could also gauge when it was safe to leave home to bunk school once my mother and step-father had left for work.

My experiences with drugs and alcohol were escalating alarmingly fast, but that wasn't my only issue.

Chapter 5

I HAVE ALWAYS BEEN SCARED to be alone.

In my relationships with men, especially, I have been desperate to feel wanted, safe, protected and, most importantly, loved. Indicative of my low self-esteem and profound fear of rejection are the physically and emotionally abusive relationships I encountered as a teenager and young woman, which at times led to suicidal tendencies and which had me rushing from one disturbed relationship to the next. My relationships were always so intense and dangerously passionate, and I suppose I thrived on that: the short tempers and the violent jealous streaks.

Ironically, the so-called "bad boys" I was so insanely attracted to from the age of thirteen were also the men I felt most safe with, because I felt they could protect me. Actually, I needed protection from myself.

For a very long time, I placed my value as a woman in all the wrong places, but perhaps that wasn't the problem: it was my own lack of self-worth. How I felt about myself depended on what the men I dated thought about me or made me feel. If there was infidelity on a boyfriend's part, then I felt it was because I wasn't good enough, that I was unwanted.

When I look at why my relationships each took a turn for the worse or completely dissolved right before my eyes, I'm forced to face the uncomfortable question on how I contributed to my own problems. And I suppose I felt it was too much of a responsibility to give myself the time and space to heal from each relationship – it was much easier to venture into a new relationship after a failed one.

And there is something else I have come to understand, too; baggage I have carried into every one of my relationships.

When I was a child, my dad could do no wrong in my eyes, but I have come to realise that it was his passivity that was so destructive to me. It had me believing that if I could find someone like him, but someone willing to play a more active role in loving and protecting me, I could change myself to make him stay. There has always been a template for the type of man I have wanted for myself, based completely on the one man whose recognition I have always sought: my father.

But that man left a very long time ago.

——◆——

I had dated Leo since I was in primary school and he was in high school, and at that time in my life it had all been innocently interesting.

But, at the age of fifteen, I lost my virginity in a back room of another boyfriend's studio apartment, in walking distance from my home in Observatory.

The guy was older than me and a musician, and my deflowering wasn't anything I had planned: he had grown tired of me refusing him and once I knew of his intentions I simply closed my eyes, listened to the Michael Speaks album that was playing in the background, and waited until it was over. My boyfriend was a popular performer in those days, and my mother had been managing his R&B group from the cottage outside her Observatory home, which operated as an office. From the first time I heard him sing, I was putty in his hands – I felt lucky that he'd chosen me among all the other girls I knew were dying for his attention.

Little did I know that they too had caught his roving eye.

With him, I found it so difficult to say no, and he always had his way with me. I didn't fear the man but I felt forced to have sexual intercourse with him whenever he wanted, wherever he wanted – even, sometimes, with my mother and step-father in the next room. In my underdeveloped thinking, I somehow believed that meant he loved me and wanted to get closer to me.

Chapter 6

I MET CASEY ONE EVENING AT A club called Enigma in Illovo, which my cousins and I would frequent almost every weekend. We called ourselves "The Chronic Sisters", and although we always arrived at the club as a posse of young girls – of which I was the youngest – I was always off doing my own thing. When I was grounded by my mother, I would bribe our gardener with a few cigarettes so that he wouldn't say anything when I snuck out. He'd even help me out of the house, depending on how hefty the bribe was.

My cousins and I would attend the university bashes at Wits, and we were also often at Club Enigma on Friday nights – except for when my mother or any of her friends happened to arrive there as well, in which case we had no option but to leave.

In those days I was into wearing baggy jeans, and sometimes I could have sworn I was a boy trapped in a girl's body. I always wore a white vest under my shirts, and I would "sag" my jeans and wear them so low that my boxers were exposed. I enjoyed playing with my pocket knife and the knuckle dusters I'd bought at Bruma Lake, and I could often be found getting new piercings in my nose or ears at one of the stalls there. I wore my braids quite long, inspired mostly by Boom Shaka and Jossie Harris of The Fly Girls on *In Living Colour*, whose music videos I loved.

Naturally, I had my teenage crushes on popular hip-hop artists and rappers. I listened to the music of 2Pac, Nas, Jay-Z, OutKast, Fugees, Lil' Kim, Mobb Deep, Snoop Dogg, Foxy Brown and Da Brat until it was coming out of my ears, and I enjoyed writing down the lyrics to songs I felt were talking to me. I wrote down poetry and my thoughts and feelings in a couple of journals I kept hidden in my bedroom.

And so there on Club Enigma's staircase on a particular night in 1996, while my cousins and friends danced the night away, I had one of the most intense moments of my teenage years when I had a sexually charged conversation with Casey. At only sixteen years old, I fell head over heels in love with this twenty-something Zimbabwean-born rapper, his talk and game so smooth it literally made the hairs on the back of my neck stand up. I was attracted to his rough look, but mostly to his sense of directness and command.

When I met Casey, I had just broken up with the boyfriend who had taken my virginity. My ex had been strict with me, and it had got to the point where his possessiveness was no longer cute, because I could do no right in his eyes. The verbal abuse had progressed into physical abuse and I had had enough of being punished – his infidelity, obsessions and the emotional decapitation he had caused had all become too much, and I had decided to move on.

Soon after my first encounter with Casey I began to spend almost every waking moment with him at his place in Yeoville. Along with my cousins and brothers, I was still at Sacred Heart College, but I was never a diligent student and school had never interested me enough for me to make an effort. I was in standard seven, but I soon started trading school days for excursions to Casey's place – and the bulk of my weekdays were soon being spent lying naked in his arms on his bed in Yeoville.

I had a measure of independence by then, because I had a weekend job at the Levi Strauss store in Sandton City. With the money I was earning – fifteen rand an hour – I could afford to pay for public transport to go see Casey, and I used a meter taxi to commute to work and back on the weekends and on during school holidays, when I worked overtime.

Leaving Casey was always unbearable. I grew so close to him in just a few weeks and I could barely keep a dry eye whenever we parted ways. Even years later it was difficult to listen to our song, "Why I love you so much" by Monica – and not because I was pained in any way over the cause of our break-up. It was because it reminded me how unbelievably happy I had been at some points in our relationship. He would put the song on repeat for me whenever I was at his place – such a romantic gesture, I thought. Because he shared his place with a friend, Casey and I spent most of our quality time in his bedroom. But to me it didn't really matter who else was around – all I ever wanted was just to be with him and to love him.

Somehow, though, being together was never written in the stars. He wanted something else.

One late afternoon we heard faint footsteps coming across the wooden floors from the front door, heading towards Casey's bedroom. The door was unlocked for a change, and suddenly on the other end of his door handle stood a tall, much older, coloured woman. It wasn't until the words, "You pig," escaped her mouth that the nature of his relationship with this woman very quickly became apparent.

Leaving me naked on the bed, Casey and his girlfriend hastily disappeared out of the bedroom, and from the other side of the wall I heard him say in desperation, "Don't worry about her – she's just a kid." When she returned to the bedroom – with Casey running after her – she was pointing a gun at me.

To this day I cannot recall the words we exchanged, or how I got a hold of the gun Casey kept near his bed. Thank goodness neither of us actually pulled a trigger; instead, we found ourselves thrashing each other on the floor, with Casey standing in disbelief at what he had caused. He must have gotten hold of the guns, but it was half an hour before he managed to pull me off her. As she stormed out of the bedroom, I pulled my clothes back on. I was so angry that he hadn't told me he was seeing someone else, and furious that he had not protected me.

I managed to get as far as the pathway leading to the street from his block of flats before he caught up with me. He tore at the strap of my backpack as a way of stopping me from going, but I left any way. I was genuinely hurt by his dishonesty and so incredibly upset that he had ruined what I felt was the perfect relationship. I was consumed with emotion and it felt like a nightmare.

I wanted my dream back.

Chapter 7

For weeks after our fallout I didn't feel like myself. My afternoons became monotonous: I'd come home, have some scrambled eggs, and then go to sleep. I had hardly ever spoken about Casey to my friends at school because he had been my little secret.

I didn't know that I was about to discover a bigger secret than I could ever have imagined.

I wasn't the type to monitor my menstrual cycle and, at first, missing my period just didn't register. Slowly, though, it began to dawn on me that I might actually be pregnant – at sixteen years old.

The next time I called Casey (from my bedroom on my favourite lip-shaped phone) would be to tell him that I thought I was pregnant. He quickly told me he would call me back, and he hung up. It wasn't too long before my phone rang again, and Casey gave me the number of a place he said I should go to. Without saying so, it was clear he wanted me to terminate my unplanned pregnancy. Looking back, I'm not sure – if I had – that he would even have offered his moral support. I could be wrong.

But our relationship was officially over with that last conversation.

———

Days, weeks and months went by and I took comfort in a friendship I developed with a hardworking Capricorn who was seven years my senior.

Like with Casey, I met my Capricorn at Club Enigma when he'd come over to introduce himself while I was sitting on a dark-leather couch. He was American with Jewish heritage – tall, light skinned and unthinkably handsome – and some of the other girls and one of my cousins had already tried to catch his interest (regardless of who had seen him first). At the end of the evening, though, it was in fact his friend who walked away with my number. Capricorn's friend and I began a brief relationship – which ended when I discovered not only that had he forgotten to inform me he was already in a relationship, but that he was about to get married.

Capricorn and I initially spent some time talking over the phone when he would call me all the way from Botswana. In no time I was completely over his friend.

Not too long into our friendship, Capricorn declared his uncontrollable feelings for me – so sweet and unblemished – and we began a four-year relationship. Two months after my break-up with Casey, I found myself at the ticket counter at

Rotunda Junction in downtown Johannesburg.

———•+•———

"I hope your family knows that you are travelling to Botswana," the lady at the counter said to me once she'd looked at my passport and issued my bus ticket.

I was set, though, and utterly determined to find my way to my Capricorn, who was living in Gaborone at the time. I had sworn my cousins to secrecy after informing them of where I was heading. Up until then, we'd only seen each other on the weekends that he'd made it to Johannesburg. I was still a part-time shop assistant at Levi Strauss on the weekends, so when he let me know that he was driving down to be with me, I'd booked us into a hotel minutes away from Sandton City – a toss-up between the nearby Don Apartments or Trafalgar Apartments. I would check into the hotel early and prep myself for his arrival. By the time he walked into the hotel room I would always be uncontrollably nervous, but excited to have him right there with me, and not just in my head as I imagined after our daily phone calls.

Now, the bus couldn't get me there soon enough, and I couldn't wait to have his arms around me. I spent the entire trip fantasising about what it would be like once we saw each other.

In Gaborone he kept to his word and there he was at the station waiting for me. My heart skipped a beat and smiled.

Gaborone was unbearably humid during that November, and I remember how he would ask me every now and then if he should put blocks of ice from the freezer into the air conditioning for me. Such a gentleman, it was gestures like this that I loved so much about him – such attention to detail – and the art he made of making love. Back in those days a brother was called "fine", and that's what I thought of this man, with his Jewish nose, big eyes (with contacts that made him look like he was constantly surprised), moustache and goatee, which he regularly groomed – I loved facial hair on men. His rapper-like demeanor completed his swag. Beneath those oversized hoodies and tees, baggy jeans and Timberlands was a man whose genuine attentiveness won me over a million times – he was so romantic and earned himself the biggest place in my heart for a very long time.

"There's a song I want you to hear," he said once we'd settled in at his place from the bus station.

"For You" by Kenny Lattimore came on, and I was immensely moved by the song he had picked and wanted me to listen to, especially the last line, that went something like "only for me". I felt so special and loved. That song became one of our favourite ballads.

———

On the second or third day of my stay in Gaborone, my mother called on his phone and told me to return home at once. I declined, but the situation was out of my hands: it wasn't her threatening to charge my Capricorn with statutory rape that ultimately sent me home, but his request that I leave before things got any worse.

I thought that my mother was simply trying to make my life miserable. For a very long time it was difficult for me to understand that she was trying to protect me.

The next day I was on the bus. I was to travel back with a cousin of Capricorn's, and I was miserable and crying on the inside. At the boarder gate I noticed a policeman holding a clipboard speaking to people in the queue. It was only when he got fairly close to me that I understood what he was saying.

"Are you Zoleka Mandela?"

When I confirmed that I was, he told me to collect all my belongings and follow him. I parted ways with Capricorn's cousin and was loaded into a police van and taken by two cops to Mafikeng.

There I was kept in an office, questioned about my whereabouts and lectured on how irresponsible it had been of me to travel to Botswana. My family was worried, I was told.

My father and cousin arrived and drove me back to Johannesburg. Perhaps they were all just glad that I was back home safely, because I didn't get the scolding or punishment I was expecting.

Chapter 8

BACK IN 1991, WHEN I WAS eleven, my mother and grandmother had hosted an *ukuthomba* ceremony for me to mark my transition into womanhood. With my back to the maroon-painted brick walls of number 8115, I had sat on a single chair that had been brought outside, and faced a crowd of people from our community and *ooDlomo*, the members of our clan, the Thembu nation. They had gathered in their numbers in the early evening, my grandmother and my mother welcoming them. The women's shoulders were draped with blankets, scarves or towels, and they wore cotton or silk scarves and other appropriate headgear for the evening.

Two months earlier I had woken up to use the bathroom,

and it wasn't until I'd got up – dressed in my usual white vest and yellow-and-grey sleeping shorts – that I'd noticed blood on the sheets. I remember the shock. I'd quickly gathered the linen and the clothes I was wearing, secretly hoping it would all just go away. My mother had never spoken to me about sex or menstruating or anything to do with my teenage body – in those days it was taboo, and very few families discussed these things. So, by the time my passage into womanhood had begun, nothing about it felt right or normal.

It was so awkward that I hid it for two whole months. I was so ashamed, and I couldn't talk to anyone about it – and even mentioning the subject to my girlfriends at school would have been far too embarrassing. I felt as if I had done something so wrong. Having stolen sanitary towels from my grandmother's bathroom I was unsure of how to dispose of them and had tried to hide them beneath my grandmother's cosmetic bag – and this, of course, is how my grandmother discovered that I was having my periods. I remember how concerned she was about how I'd struggled to manage during those two awful months. I'd felt so much better once my parents had been informed. My father had driven me to the store at what was then the Maponya Centre in Orlando to purchase my own sanitary towels, and because I was too embarrassed to buy them myself, he'd gone in and then returned with a pink packet of New Freedom sanitary towels.

For some reason my father wasn't present at the *ukuthomba* ceremony, where my grandmother and my mother proudly announced to those who had gathered that I was officially a woman. I don't recall it being a proud moment for me. I remember feeling so embarrassed about being pushed into the spotlight, with all these woman there staring at me. A sheep was slaughtered for me, and I was made to taste some of the gall bladder, which was extremely bitter and which was placed on my head afterwards. My grandmother then gave me five thousand rand as a gift, although neither of us can recall what we ever did with it.

She says I kept repeating the words that she was directing at me: "This is your key to womanhood, to the adult world." In retrospect, I wish I had written in my diary about that day: I can now see that it was an important rite of passage, steeped in culture and tradition, and it means so much to me now that I experienced it.

But perhaps I took my grandmother's remark about being in the adult world a little too seriously.

I was sixteen years old, it was a few months after I had returned from my Botswana trip, and things were beginning to change. In the first month of standard eight, as I sat in class, the desk I shared with a friend started to move. My friend asked me why it was moving, and I quickly dismissed the question. But out the corner of my eye I could see the baby kick to the left of my growing belly, and I moved my chair back to give me enough room to lean forward.

At that point in my school life I was participating in quite a few extra murals, including basketball, hockey and netball. The school change room became my worst nightmare. I no longer changed for sports with the rest of the girls. Instead, I'd change in one of the toilet cubicles so no one could see the tattered elasticated corset I was using to try and flatten my stomach.

I was desperate and I needed help. I was struggling to conceal my pregnancy and I knew it was only a matter of time before it was discovered.

In May of that year, I gathered all the money I had and called a Maxi Taxi to come and collect me from home. Sis' Hazel was a domestic worker whom I had developed an extreme attachment to during the time she worked for my mother and looked after us in Observatory. She had recently found a new job after she had stopped working for my mother, and I asked the taxi to take me there.

She had been the first person I had told about my incident in the studio down the road from the house. I remember how upset she was with me when I told her I had lost my virginity. That day, I'd sat on a chair holding onto my knees with my head buried in my lap while Sis' Hazel cooked in the kitchen. I hadn't got the reaction I wanted from her that time – I was hoping she would come and hold me, but she'd been angry. Nevertheless, we were extremely close and my first instinct was to go to her now that I knew I was pregnant.

Sis' Hazel was cleaning up in the sitting room in her new employer's home when I shared with her the news of my pregnancy. She stopped what she was doing and looked at me. She knew what this meant and she begged me to return home, but my future had everything to do with the foetus I was carrying, and I knew I couldn't. I had no money, and only the school uniform I was wearing for clothes, and I didn't know what I was going to do after leaving her workplace. She made me something to eat and told me that I looked tired and should go take a nap in the maid's quarters while she finished cleaning the house.

To her credit, that must have been the only way she could do what she had to: as I lay on her bed a while later, contemplating my next move, I heard the sound of high-heeled footsteps. My Aunt Zenani had come to take me home, and I had never been so relieved and happy to see her in my life.

41

———◆———

I had managed to hide my pregnancy from my family, my friends and my Capricorn for eight whole months. I hadn't known I was that far along until I heard my aunt Zenani's gynaecologist mention to her and my grandmother that I was eight months pregnant. My family and friends were informed just a month before the birth.

"Zozo, do you see what you have done? You have gone and made me a grandfather," my father had said passively.

My mother hadn't spoken to me for weeks after she'd found out.

It was also then, when I was eight months pregnant with Casey's child, that I'd told my Capricorn. I had managed to hide my pregnancy from him too. He would spend the next four years of our relationship raising Zenani as his own flesh and blood.

———◆———

But my Capricorn was not with me in hospital when I gave birth. On that morning, I didn't even know I was in labour. After countless trips to the bathroom while my brothers were getting ready for school, my waters broke. I wasn't exactly aware of what was happening until I was already in the car with both my mother and step-father. My mother told me to tell her each time I felt pain in my womb. She offered me her hand to squeeze, and after about the third or fourth squeeze she said I was definitely having contractions. My step-father drove us to the hospital.

In my hospital bed, I would start off sitting upright at the head of the bed, but would be lying in agony at the foot of the bed after a contraction or two.

"You can cry if you want to," my grandmother said as I squeezed her hand. I never did cry, though, and when I think about it, I realise that that must have been the first and last time my grandmother ever told me it was okay to cry. "Never cry in public," was what she usually always told us.

At Park Lane Clinic in Johannesburg, after five hours of labour, I had an emergency Caesarean. I had barely dilated four centimeters when the gynaecologist burst into the room to inform me that the medical staff were going to prepare me for an epidural – I urgently needed to get into theatre due to foetal distress.

On the operating table, my gynaecologist told me to look into his prescription glasses if I wanted to see exactly how my child would be born. I did not take my eyes of his glasses. When I finally did, it was to watch the nurse rush my baby out of the delivery room to ensure that all was well. At 12:07, I heard my newborn baby girl take her first breath and cry for the first time. My mother left the theatre to be with her granddaughter and I was so touched by that gesture after the weeks of silence.

My baby weighed a healthy 3.615 kilograms, and I was later told that her umbilical cord had been wrapped around her neck, decreasing her heart rate.

———•—•———

On 9 June 1997, at the tender age of seventeen, I gave birth to the only best friend I will ever know, Zenani Zanethemba Nomasonto Mandela. Even that early, my firstborn and only daughter's birth altered my entire existence. I knew then what I have known ever since: my life began the moment she chose me as her mother.

Nothing in the world mattered as much as my baby did.

From the moment that I left the hospital I would spend the next few years dedicating myself to her.

For too short a time, I didn't know how to do anything else but to love and care for her.

Chapter 9

By the time I got home with Zenani, an aunt had prepared my room for our arrival, and it wasn't too long afterwards that my Capricorn came to meet this amazing soul who had given meaning to my life.

One night, during those early days, my mother came into my bedroom to check on Zenani. She says that she found me fast asleep in my bed, and there was my Capricorn, exhausted, with Zenani in his arms as he sat next to me on the bed, his back resting against the headboard, his head drooping on his shoulder. He'd taken over because he wanted me to get some rest. Deeply touched by his concern, my mother had insisted that he spend the night.

After that, he would often stay with us on weekends

when he drove in from Botswana. And when he did, we were perfect. For a change, we weren't smoking weed in some hotel room and getting high while we made love.

We were a perfect little family.

———•——

Very expectant with Zenani, I'd dropped out of school in May 1997, and spent the rest of that year looking after her. I resumed high school in 1998 at Damelin Eden College in Braamfontein. Technically, I should have repeated standard eight, but because I had already repeated standard two, I was more worried about the age of my peers than the amount of work that would be required of me. Luckily, I managed to be promoted to standard nine, and I went on to matriculate the following year.

My Capricorn was quite popular at my school and whenever he could, he would collect me from school in his White KIA Sportage, rap music blasting. One of the greatest rappers I knew locally, my Capricorn was also an innovative producer. He was also the only man I saw myself marrying.

My Capricorn, Zenani and I did everything together. A trip we made to Cape Town as a family was more than perfect. The three of us visited Green Market Square, where he bought me the gold-and-cubic-zirconia ring that I wore on my wedding finger as a promise ring. I really believed in the promise that we would one day marry.

When we went to visit his family in Sacramento, California, I boarded a flight and eventually arrived into the care of his maternal aunt and cousin, who picked me up from the airport. During our holiday there I stayed in their home, in a bedroom I shared with him. I loved playing the role if not of his wife, then his long-term partner. We belonged to each other and everyone knew it.

The year 2000 marked the unexpected end of our relationship, leaving me broken down, hurt and angry. For ages I would still cringe at the mere mention of his name, because usually it was followed by the thought that he was The One.

———

Four years together.

Although the strain of our long-distance relationship had played a major role, at the end of our relationship I questioned whether in any of the four years we'd been together he'd ever been faithful to me. All that time I had trusted him implicitly, and I'd never felt the need to look over my shoulder. I was left feeling rejected, disrespected and unwanted.

And there was something else. After my Capricorn and I broke up, I needed to function like a single parent for the first time.

Chapter 10

ALTHOUGH THERE WERE THINGS FOR which I couldn't forgive my Capricorn for many years to come, I didn't make my life any easier with the reckless decisions I made as I desperately tried to numb my pain.

One in particular was the relationship I began with a good friend at the time of my break-up with my Capricorn. And that wasn't the only unhealthy relationship I entered into.

I began my affair with cocaine at the same time as I began one with my Libra, who'd just broken up with my cousin after they'd spent three years together. My Libra was a musician too, and he invited me over to his studio one night, along with another friend. I had gone because I didn't want to be anywhere where my Capricorn could find me for fear that I would take him back, but he had called me on my cellphone anyway, parked outside the studio. It was just a few days after our break-up – I was still so emotionally sore, angry and deeply disappointed.

And that's the state I was in when I was introduced to cocaine. My Libra and his friend had been busy working on their music while I sat on the couch opposite the recording booth. There was an assortment of alcoholic drinks on the coffee table, and I helped myself. During that studio session, I saw the guys use cocaine, and I remember how, after I'd asked to try some, I'd quickly felt this incredibly good feeling come over me.

I must have used cocaine with them all night because the sunrise found me naked on the studio's balcony outside, in full view of the neighbours, with my Libra telling me how beautiful I looked with the sunrise behind me and that I just needed to learn to let go.

That's all it took: one drug-infested "romantic" moment which had me hooked not only on cocaine, but also on a man who would get me higher than the drug he'd introduced me to. After that night I was addicted to both.

Before long I was making a pretence of being dropped off to attend my Psychology lectures at the Midrand Graduate Institute. My grandmother had assigned a driver to me, but as soon as he had left, my Libra would pull up and we'd steal some time together at his sister's place in Lone Hill. He would drop me back at Midrand in time for my driver to collect me.

"You two are dangerously in love," my mother said to him once, referring to our many fights, break-ups and obsessions with each other.

She was right.

But my Capricorn was still on my mind.

And, in reality, despite moving on to the next relationship, I was still just running away from my pain.

Strangely enough, after our break-up, my Capricorn had tried everything to get me to take him back, but at the time my ego was still bruised and I'd rejected him. Months later, and in a pit of despair in my relationship with my Libra, I'd called him, wanting us to try again.

I hadn't expected that by that time my Capricorn would have already moved on. And it hurt all the more.

I lost myself with my Libra.

One evening my Libra and I were at Innesfree Park, fooling around outside the car. Police had been patrolling the area and had stopped when they'd seen his car. They'd watched us from a distance for quite some time, and by the time they shone their headlights in our direction, we were engaged in sexual intercourse. One of the policemen told us to grab our clothes, which were all over the place, and to leave immediately. We got off lightly after a warning, but I would be lying if I said there weren't other incidents of that nature. Dangerously, irresponsibly, criminally in love.

My Libra and I.

Sometimes it felt like a sin *not* to be together and I was so attracted to how insanely my Libra loved me back.

We were so much alike, and I was almost a hundred per cent sure he felt the exactly same way.

I had stayed in touch with my Leo for years through my teens, and now in my twenties, I started seeing him again. Things were always on and off with my Libra and it didn't help much that we were banned from seeing each other by our families – especially because he had been in a serious relationship with my cousin. There were periods during which we didn't see each other for months at a time.

And you can't bash something without trying it out first, right?

Wrong.

I tried magic mushrooms for the first time in Orange Grove. It was a weekend night and I'd stepped out of the busy club and gone to sit with my Leo in his car. Parked directly opposite the club, he reached into what looked like a clear-plastic sandwich bag and grabbed a few mushrooms, which I put in my mouth, chewed briefly and swallowed. Just as baffling as the taste that the dried-up mushrooms left on my tongue is the mystery of how I found my way back to my cousins, and how we got home. I don't recall anything that happened after I'd ingested the hallucinogenic drug, but a cousin said they had looked for me after I'd disappeared.

While everyone else stuck to alcohol and weed, like a typical maverick I was trying whatever came my way.

Depending on Leo's group's performances, where each gig was and how long it took to leave, I would sometimes find myself in random hotel rooms waiting for him to knock. Because I was so relieved that he even pitched up, I would pretend I wasn't bothered about how long he always made me wait – after all, he had chosen me to come home to, even if "home" that night was some dingy, used-up hotel room.

Spurred on by Ecstasy, we could not keep our hands off each other and engaged in extensive sexual sessions, which I pined for when the drug had worn off. We regularly engaged in risky sexual behaviour in unsafe places – in public toilets, on highways outside his car and in full view of oncoming traffic. And for my part, I didn't want it any other way than to feel desired by him – my "Ruff Neck", with his erratic and unpredictable nature. It was beastly, and it went too far when he burnt my lower back with the cigarette he was smoking while we were having sexual intercourse.

I don't recall feeling scared then, but it scares me now to think of how many times I put myself at risk, and how many times I was spared. In my relationship with my Leo I saw things I should never have seen, and I allowed things to happen that shouldn't have happened – images in my head that I still find difficult to believe.

The truth was that for some reason my feelings had changed, and I suddenly couldn't stand him. If it wasn't something he'd said, it was something he'd done; if it wasn't his deodorant that was making me sick to my stomach, then it was the sound of his voice over the intercom when he came to visit or when we spoke on the phone.

Something was not right. And everything I ate left a horrible taste in my mouth.

One day I found myself making a quick detour down one of the aisles at the chemist – trying to evade a cousin-in-law who also happened to be in the shop – so that I could grab a pregnancy test. I paid for it and shoved it in my bag, but not before my cousin-in-law had caught a whiff of the trouble I suspected I was in. I had missed my period again, and it was fraying on the edges of my sanity.

As it happened, while I had managed to purchase the pregnancy test, I hadn't been very successful in concealing it, because my cousin-in-law later made mention of the contents of my bag.

At home, I followed the instructions word for word, preparing myself for the outcome. I didn't know anything about false-positive tests, or having to purchase at least two to three tests just to make sure.

But it didn't matter anyway.

I was pregnant.

I told Bryan the news one morning as he sat on the bed in the bedroom of a place he shared in Buccleuch. Although

I'd known for a few weeks by then, it had all been a bit too surreal. I'd been on an emotional rollercoaster – from excitement about having another baby, to extreme worry over the financial rut Bryan was in.

Zenani was only five years old, and although I was working two jobs, they didn't pay enough for me to take care of both my babies alone. I was lucky that my mother and maternal grandparents had been able to help me financially, but I also wanted to be able to support my family myself.

Since I'd made my discovery, though, my relationship with Bryan had gone from bad to worse, and although he'd initially been ecstatic at receiving the news, things didn't get any better as my pregnancy progressed.

Bryan usually called me from a public phone at a shop that was walking distance from his rental. Five months into the pregnancy, I received a series of disturbing phone calls from him: he was accusing me of having an affair with one of his friends, and he wanted nothing to do with my unborn baby and me.

For the rest of the pregnancy, Bryan became a complete stranger to me. It didn't matter how many times I tried to convince him otherwise – he had convinced himself that I had had an affair with a friend of his who, to this day, I have never met. The "friend" had apparently been jealous of our relationship and had fabricated the whole story in the hope that it would break us up. It worked, but the person who really lost out here was my unborn child, who wouldn't know his father until much later.

At some point many months later, Bryan apologised, but the insults, unforgiveable hurt and harassment he had subjected me to were too much. I kept a safe distance from him, leaving us the relative strangers we are today. He calls and visits his son when he wants to, but no more than that.

Chapter 12

On 21 November 2002, I gave birth to my second born and my strength, Zwelami Zendj Mafanyana Mandela. Zwelami was born at Park Lane Clinic at 3:36 in the afternoon, weighing 3.2 kilograms.

At twenty-two years old, I was a single parent of two.

The first thing Zwelami did once he was placed on my chest was look me dead in the eyes, almost as if to make sure it was me who he had chosen. I was taken aback at how he stared at me for what felt like the longest time before his gaze shifted away. He had long black hair, only just shorter than the hair his sister had had. In the coming days, I would grin every time I saw the side parting the nurses gave him after his daily bath.

Due to my previous emergency Caesarean, my gynaecologist had recommended that I have an elective Caesarean section this time, believing my son would be too large for the vaginal birth I had wanted. Although I was feeling ill from the medication, I couldn't wait for Zenani to arrive at the hospital after school to meet her brother – and with my two children tucked in my arms, I felt like a complete family.

———————

Zenani and Zwelami became inseparable and even from the age of five, Zenani became like a second mother to her brother. She always loved babies and small children, and she always got her own way with them, constantly faffing around the little children she met. She had her own way of relating to Zwelami, and sometimes I'd have to ask her to please speak to her brother whenever I felt I wasn't getting through to him.

She did an exceptional job looking after her brother – a better one than I did, at the time.

———————

I used cocaine on and off for the first ten years of the millennium.

While I was carrying and during the two years that I breast fed Zwelami I managed to refrain from drugs, alcohol or cigarettes, as I had with Zenani, but as much as I didn't miss them during that time, like a jilted lover they always seemed to find their way back.

Other than when I was pregnant or breastfeeding, I craved my drugs as much as I craved whatever man I was dating. Being in a relationship made me feel that I mattered to someone, that I was special. Sex made me feel better about myself, just as cocaine did, and it continued in a cycle: the relationships doomed to failure by the drugs and alcohol which we *thought* kept us together, but which actually tore us apart; the intense and passionate sexual encounters that followed violent and vulgar fights. The risks I was taking then have me wondering just how the heck I was lucky enough to have survived it all.

For as long as I could remember, though, I had been walking around with an emptiness inside me so big that no man, drink or drug could fill it.

———◆———

For my twenty-third birthday I hosted an "Oscar Night" party on my mother's tennis court. At that point I was still quite seriously involved with my Libra, but I met a guy there, "J". Although I don't recall thinking much of him then, much later, after my break up with Libra, we started dating.

J was a Zulu man, like my ex who had broken my virginity. He was overtly friendly and would visit me at my office and play with my son. Because he always seemed genuine, I thought he was sweet. He was tall, muscular, dark skinned, incredibly handsome and he could wear the heck out of a suit. And he was persistent too, because after all the visiting, he one day paid me an unexpected visit at home, and demanded that I walk hand in hand with him to his car, where he stole our first kiss. I was surprised, but I loved how it felt.

You didn't have to know who he was to sense the danger around this man. J had his hands in everything, but he was notorious for drug dealing and handling "damage control" – being paid to hurt people who had crossed him. I knew he had a violent streak, because one night he returned to his car to fetch his gun after my cousin-in-law's friend had said something along the lines of what was I doing with someone like him. The comment upset J greatly. One evening we had both used cocaine and were on our way to buy drinks when he stopped at a house in Buccleuch. He had noticed that his friend was in a fight there, and he left the car to help him.

"Baby, sit in the driver's seat in case you have to take off," he said.

As much as it sounded like a movie, I did as he told me and watched from the driver's seat. There was something exciting about the fact that he had his friend's back and I felt he always had mine.

But you don't take notice of the warning signs when you are racing headlong into addiction.

In those days, it wasn't unusual for me to be in the company of men; I seldom hung out with women. In the Buccleuch house where J and I would watch pornography and have sex, there were always men drinking, using or watching television, and I didn't feel uncomfortable – although, of course, once cocaine is in your system everyone around you is suddenly your best friend.

One night a group of men walked in. I was walking into the kitchen to get myself another beer, which I downed one after the other in those days, and one of the men said he wanted me for the night.

As far as he was concerned, I might as well have been a prostitute in a brothel.

J was quick to answer him in his strong Zulu accent – he said I was "his" and they would have problems if the guy carried on. For some reason, him letting everyone in the room know that I "belonged" to him made me feel deeply cared for. Although I now wonder what, if he cared that much for me, I was doing there in the first place.

But I went there and anywhere else he wanted me to go, because wherever I was with him, I felt safe. I loved his power and I loved the fear I sensed in others when they talked about how he operated in the long-term disputes he had with his nemesis. I loved that he took my body as he pleased and for however long he wanted. There were so many times when, under normal circumstances, I would have felt vulnerable, but he always made me feel like his top priority and that I could call on him for protection at any time.

He made me feel cared for, he felt right for me, but he was never mine.

—◆—

"Should you tell her or should I?" my two cousins were saying as they walked into my cottage one day. "Babe, I think you need to sit down for this."

The lump in my throat was making it difficult to swallow; my heart was pounding. My cousin handed me a copy of "Shwashwi", the celeb section of the *Sunday World*. In it was a picture of my Libra and his ex-girlfriend, also a musician, sitting at a table at a function we'd been supposed to attend together. I hadn't gone because he'd told me some lie about why he had to attend it alone.

The article said it all: they'd been together for ten years and were as happy as can be.

It was 2005, and my Libra and I had been together on and off for five years (and before that he'd been with my cousin for three). I'd seen other people during the times that we were broken up, had even had a pregnancy, but somehow we'd always got back together. This time confirmed my worst fear: we would never find our way back to each other again.

Moreover, why had the world been alerted to the end of our relationship before I was? Was I not worthy of the truth?

I was devastated.

"I think you should move on with your life," my Libra said to me over the phone when I called for an explanation. On the other eight times he'd cheated on me I'd got the "I'm sorry, baby" and I'd taken him back. But this time was different.

In disbelief and indescribably hurt, I called my grandmother, not knowing what else to do. Although it was me who needed the harsh talk, there was a part of me that wanted her to talk some sense into him.

"Darling, I told you never to depend on a man," she said.

I had just been dumped by my Libra over the phone, but right then I felt that I was an even bigger disappointment to my grandmother.

She was right, though. I'd been dependent on him for so many things, especially because he had insisted I quit my job at Cell C and focus on my studies while he took care of me financially. But what I couldn't understand was: if I'd done everything he'd ever wanted of me, why was it me who had been dumped? He'd even begun talking about lobola negotiations.

I was confused and hurt, and it took me another five years to get my Libra completely out of my system. No other relationship I had could never measure up. Even though it failed so miserably, I felt at the time that being with my Libra had been the best thing about me. For a very long time I strongly believed that my Libra had ruined all men for me.

In 2007 I moved with my son and daughter out of my mother's house and into my Aunt Zenani's five-bedroomed home in Morningside. I was still studying part time at the Midrand Graduate Institute, and had worked as a personal assistant to a filming company's CEO before resigning to focus on my studies.

Zenani turned ten and Zwelami turned five that year, and I spent as much time with them as my studies allowed – helping them with their homework, cooking their meals and playing. It was a great year for us to bond. Without a relationship to focus on, I called myself "Desperate Housewife Without the Husband".

Chapter 13

I MET SEKOATI IN 2008.

I had walked down the stairs of my aunt's home to find him sitting on one of the dining-room chairs – this light-skinned, tall and good-looking man with dreadlocks tied at the back of his head. His looks were refreshing, and I remember feeling something for him even early on, even though I was still obsessively in love with my then-boyfriend, my Malawian Pisces, who I'd met when we'd both worked at Cell C. It wasn't until much later that Sekoati would confess to being attracted to me from the first time he saw me walking down the stairs.

Sekoati was a friend of my Pisces, and that day my Pisces had asked him to drop us off for dinner at Adega at The

Wedge on Rivonia Road. This was to become a weekly get-together for the three of us, a routine that lasted for almost a year, during which time Sekoati went from being a complete stranger to a close and platonic friend. Sekoati was someone whose company I particularly enjoyed because I felt he understood me. He never shied away from being brutally honest, and I respected his bluntness.

My Pisces was a part-time disc jockey and was between jobs; Sekoati was a full-time actor and an upcoming musician. Their connection was the same one I shared: we were "using buddies", and when things were good they were really great, but when they were bad they were terrible. I came to need those guys like I needed my two bottles of Beyerskloof red wine followed by a gram of cocaine every evening of the week.

As the months passed, the three of us would always be found together until the time that I introduced Sekoati to a cousin of mine; they began seeing each other, even though he was in a relationship with the mother of his two children at the time. I remember driving to Innesfree Park one Sunday afternoon – us girls in the back seat of the car and the guys in the front as we drank, listened to music and used cocaine. Sekoati drove doughnuts with his car wheels, and that excited me: he wasn't afraid of anyone or anything, and he always did what he wanted.

I do remember Sekoati refusing to join us one afternoon because he said that all we did those days was use drugs. He said he was tired of snorting cocaine all the time, and I literally begged him to join us anyway because to me it didn't feel right without him there.

But the things that brought the three of us together were the very same things that would ultimately drive us apart: Cocaine. Alcohol. Addiction.

My Pisces and Sekoati owned Club Red, a very shady club located near a well-known strip club called Malasha, and, strangely enough, just two streets away from the Houghton House Addiction Recovery Centre, which I was to get to know very well two years later. At the time, though, I had just worked on a big project with my mother and I was spending a lot of my earnings on hotel rooms, restaurants, takeaways, alcohol and drugs.

It was guaranteed: wherever we went, there'd be a dealer a few minutes away for making a drop, and there was a routine to how we used the drugs. Once we'd picked them up, I would place them in my weave or in my bra in case the cops stopped us – chances were that male police officers wouldn't search me. In the car, we used our bank cards to cut the cocaine on the back of a CD, each of us eyeing the cover to check that whoever was cutting the lines was being both generous and fair as they distributed the cocaine between whoever of us wanted it. "Corner to corner, coast to coast," we'd laugh and say, especially when we would use the corner of the bank card to scoop up enough cocaine from a bag to snort.

We would each have had at least a few lines by the time we reached our destination. A club called Sunrise was a favourite spot to buy alcohol because it closed much later than all the other places. I remember how once, just as the three of us had jumped back into the car after buying some alcohol, the cops stopped their vehicle right next to our car. I was sitting in the back seat and the two policemen started searching the guys. One of them said to me, "You're lucky. If there was a female police cop here, she would be searching you right now."

I didn't get searched that night, and what they didn't know was that we were all high and that the drugs were safely in my bra, to be used not too many seconds after the coast felt clear.

Although the last few years had been anything but stable, in late 2008, my life took a turn for the worse. My youngest step-sister, Kefuoe Seakamela, just seven years old, tragically lost her life while swimming at Sacred Heart College, a school my brothers, most of my cousins and I had gone to.

I was working in the dining room, which we used as an events office, at my mother's house in Saxonwold when I received the call from my father. When he told me that my sister had just drowned in the school pool, I was in shock – he had to repeat himself many times before I understood what he was saying.

"Zozo, we've lost your sister," he said to me.

I remember crying uncontrollably and throwing up in the guest bathroom before we made our way to the school. When I arrived at the pool with my grandmother and mother, all of us in absolute disbelief, I found my father on the floor with his head lowered, sitting next to my sister's body. I've never seen my father look so helpless, so debilitated with pain as he struggled with the sight that was before his eyes. She was lying there in her bathing suit and you could tell that she had been in the pool for a long time. The image is as fresh in my memory as if it happened just yesterday.

By the end of that year, I had dropped out of college and began drinking quite heavily again. Although I had first indulged in cocaine years before, by now I had taken the significant step of drinking and drugging alone.

My relationship with my Pisces was getting worse.

We fought almost constantly. I'd kicked him out as often as he had left, but we'd always taken each other back. One evening we had a physical fight at one of Sekoati's Honeydew rentals (which posed as a studio, but which we really used as a space to get up to our nonsense). Empty Heineken bottles and fists were flying, and slaps were exchanged before he took my car keys, walked out of the complex and caught the first flight back home to Malawi.

The next day I got back to my grandmother's home in Soweto, where we'd been staying, and the first thing I did when I got into my bedroom was to check for his things. This time, there was not a single item of his in the room and he was nowhere to be found. We had dated for close to two years.

So I moved on to the next one.

My Pisces' departure led to an affair with Sekoati. He was the second closest person to me, and with Pisces gone, I felt like Sekoati was all I had. We dated on and off for just over two years and they were the longest two years of my life.

I remember that one night Sekoati and I had gone out for dinner at a new restaurant when we bumped into his cousin and the cousin's girlfriend, both of whom I knew and used to use with. In one of the cubicles in the restaurant the girlfriend and I did a few lines of cocaine, but it wasn't until we'd left the restaurant that I began having a bad reaction to the drugs. We pulled over to the side of the road in a woody area, and I recall throwing up and running into the veld. Later, when I'd found my way back to where the car was parked, Sekoati was there with the police, who he'd called in a panic, knowing he couldn't call my family. I didn't know where my shoes were and I returned home covered in dirt and dry leaves.

Our friendship was based on drugs and alcohol but, even so, Sekoati and I were so much better as friends.

I hated him. I loved him. I resented him.

Chapter 14

I HAD MOVED BETWEEN MY mother's house and my grandmother's house on too many occasions. I found it extremely difficult to live by either of their rules, so if one upset me, I would move in with the other.

I never realised how the instability affected my children.

My mother's rental, or "Athol" as we called it, seemed initially to be perfectly suited to a large family like ours. It had a number of identical bedrooms, and each came with a mini fridge, glass lamp shades, a single brown leather stool and two dark-brown bedside tables on each side of a large bed. It was supposed to be a family home, but we seldom ever had just our family visiting or living there. In the house in Houghton, we had often sat chatting by the fireplace on winter evenings, and every evening we'd sat at the dinner table as a family. By contrast, Athol felt like a commune. Although we occasionally shared meals together or watched TV in the lounge, in Athol we all spent most of our time in our own comfortable rooms, where each person dictated their own set of rules.

In my own room, the rule to "Please knock before you come in" was for the sake of safety rather than a formality. If my door was locked it was because I didn't want the kids or anyone else in my family to see me using cocaine or doing something else shameful.

I always stocked my fridge with Heineken because on the weekends I would drink a six-pack for breakfast. I usually bought a case of beer at a time to ensure I could cater for my average of eighteen beers a day. When I was alone in my bedroom opposite the kids' room, it was quite typical of me to use cocaine combined with alcohol, and I was in the habit of using at least a gram or two of cocaine at a time.

———•——

On 1 June 2010 I was hospitalised for depression and attempted suicide after a drug-induced psychotic episode. The family doctor had carried my clothing bag from my bedroom at my mother's Athol home, and I was now lying in a hospital bed at Brenthurst Clinic, just a few streets from Hillbrow. For ten days I would be under my doctor's care in, of all places, the orthopaedic section, because there was an influx of patients in the other medical wards.

The doctor had been called by my mother and grandmother after I'd set my bedroom alight.

On this particular Tuesday afternoon, I'd been out with J when he suggested we try a new bag of cocaine. I seldom refused an offer: I loved the feeling as it travelled through my nostrils; I enjoyed the burn in my nose and the numbness in my gums once I'd rubbed it in with my finger. This time, though, I remember feeling somewhat unaffected because I'd only had three or four lines.

I didn't feel high by the time he'd dropped me off at home, and I had a sudden urge to smoke a cigarette. Needing to drink and smoke was an automatic response for me, almost as if I was making up for feeling too sober, having not had the luxury of unlimited cocaine.

My mother was more of a gin drinker at the time, though she would drink beer occasionally, and she kept a bottle of Tanqueray in her fridge. As soon as I got in, I went to her bedroom to check whether she had any gin in her mini fridge. I didn't even bother with a glass of tonic water as I took gulps straight from the bottle, even as I sat on the toilet.

Back in my own room, I had been opening and closing my sliding door since I'd returned home – stepping outside for a cigarette, then coming back in, only to head out immediately, craving yet another cigarette. I remember going to my bathroom with the last bit of gin and leaving the bottle there, but I can't recall when I changed into my pyjamas and gown, or why I became so thoroughly depressed and overwhelmed with such unbearable self-loathing.

I recall sitting cross-legged on the floor of my bedroom facing the door, and feeling the heat from the flames I had started. To my left stood a tall and dark figure, an apparition, a faceless man, with what looked like a coat and a hat.

This wasn't the first time I had interacted with this man. He had always had two other dark-figured men with him, and in the past I had seen them mostly at the foot of my bed. It was usually when I was in bed watching TV that I'd notice the two men – they'd be walking back and forth from my bedroom door to the sliding door to the patio on the opposite side of the room, or from the door past my closet to the bathroom. At times I had found them walking around in the kitchen. My visions had never been alarming until late one night when I'd gone into the kitchen and seen the fridge being shaken by the two men under the tallest one's orders.

This time, though, was the first time the man had given me direct orders.

He had told me to carry out his order to kill myself.

He wanted me to burn myself to death.

He had handed me the lighter and waited, and in some way I had felt compelled enough to start the fire.

Although no words were exchanged and I can't explain it, he seemed to lose patience when my hair didn't catch fire like he wanted.

I'm not sure how long after I'd set the brown bedroom carpet alight that the fumes found their way down the passage, past the last of the bedrooms to the open lounge area, where my youngest brother, Zwelabo, was sitting. He raced down the passage and kicked open my burning bedroom door, to find me on the floor swaying back and forth as if in a trance. As he was trying to speak to me, my pupils rolled back into their sockets until all he could see was the whites of my eyes. He picked me up and took me across the passage to my son and daughter's bedroom, where he lay me on a bed while everyone else rushed to my room.

At some point Zenani and Zwelami came to look at me from the door. My mother then arranged for them to stay at my Aunt Zenani's place, and I remember Zenani sticking her head into the room to tell me that she would keep checking up on me until they left.

She said she was going to take care of me, and she asked if I was okay.

"Mom, we're leaving now." The kids came in for the last time before leaving, and I remember Zenani saying that she loved me right before she gave me a hug and a kiss and said goodbye.

In no time the family doctor had come to pick me up, and by then I had found a suitcase and randomly thrown in some clothing for the hospital.

He said all the clothes I had packed that evening were black.

I was in tears leaving the house.

I was so ashamed. I hated myself for what I'd done and it scared me to think how the fire could have ended. Why hadn't I died?

I was admitted to hospital for what I thought was depression and suicidal behaviour, and I would spend the next nine days in a hospital bed being injected daily with an antidepressant and other medicines. I loved the relief of feeling numb and sleepy before dozing off for hours at a time.

In the days I spent there I became used to the nurses and the cleaning staff walking in and out my hospital room, and if it wasn't them then it was my doctor or my psychiatrist who would visit.

One afternoon, a few days before I left the hospital, I was lying asleep on top of my bed covers when I heard the voices of two mature women.

"Don't worry. She will be okay," one of them said.

I remember feeling a warmness behind me as I slept facing the window, and how it felt like I was being spooned with warmth and love. I woke up to the realisation that I was alone in the room. Perhaps I had been dreaming but those voices had seemed so real to me.

I continued watching television that afternoon and fell into a deep sleep after the nurses had given me my antidepressant shot and a sedative to help me sleep.

━━◆━━

In the early hours of 11 June 2010, I woke up to my father, my Aunt Zenani and my brother Zodwa walking into my hospital room. They told me they had come to take me home.

There had been a car accident.

My only daughter, Zenani, had been killed.

I don't remember anything else after my aunt and brother told me that. The last time I ever saw her was during that dreadful night when she had come to say goodbye after I had tried to burn myself alive.

━━◆━━

The biggest part of me died with her that June morning.

How I left the hospital room and found myself back in the room Zenani had shared with Zwelami, I do not know. But I remember lying on her bed, where the base had already been removed as per tradition, in a room filled with friends and family who had come to extend their condolences. My grandfather's medics had administered a tranquiliser to me.

Everything else is a blur.

I kept thinking: God should have taken me instead.

━━◆━━

I chose my daughter's coffin at Kupane Funerals in Soweto.

On that day I couldn't believe that I was upstairs picking a coffin while my daughter lay alone and cold in one of the rooms below me.

How does a mother who loves her child walk away from that?

At the funeral home I was given the belongings that she'd had with her in the car. She had with her so many clothes that evening, all of which were now covered in blood. In the plastic bag from Kupane Funerals was a gold-and-black Baby Phat jacket of mine that I'd never worn, but which I knew Zenani had loved.

I remember the smell of my daughter's blood following me as I carried the plastic bag with me, removed it from the car and placed it next to me in the downstairs bedroom at my grandmother's home, where I would mourn her passing.

I spent time with my daughter at the mortuary just moments before we laid her to rest on 18 June. I asked her father, Casey, who had barely ever made time to see her, to give me a moment alone with her. I hadn't seen Zenani for the whole ten days since my episode, but as soon as I walked into the mortuary, I knew exactly which coffin was my daughter's – they didn't have to tell me where she was.

I felt her.

She had sustained horrendous injuries – her face was covered because it was so badly disfigured, and my family refused to let me see her as I had seen my little sister.

At home, my father had been collecting the outfit she would be laid to rest in when I said I had forgotten to give him her shoes. He'd told me that I would only need one shoe, because my daughter's other foot had been severed at the ankle. It was only during the trial that I found out that a piece of her foot had remained in the car, and that her Samsung cellphone had never been found. I was also told that the elderly women in the family who had gone to give her her last bath were traumatised after seeing the condition the drunk-driving accident had left her in.

I know that if I had been left alone with her, I would have peeled away the material covering her face. I wanted to see for myself how bad it was, but my family tried to protect me by sparing the details of her injuries – details I would only learn for the first time during the court process, and when I accidentally saw a photograph of her body.

To this day I cry tears at the thought that I declined having her hands exposed so I could hold them because I was too scared that I would remove the wrapping that covered her head and face. Instead, I looked at them when I should have held my daughter's beautiful hands for the last time.

Chapter 15

IN THE EARLY HOURS OF THE MORNING when we laid Zenani to rest, Zwelami fell asleep in his black suit in the back seat of the combi.

I'd had to beg my eldest cousin to allow me to say goodbye to my daughter at the cemetery because I'd been told that women were not allowed to bury Zenani; that it was something for the men to do, especially with the unfortunate circumstances of her accident. But in the end I was called to join the men, and I walked to her final resting place, and kissed her coffin, and held on to it so tightly as it was being lowered into the ground. I watched it in disbelief – I would never get to see my little girl ever again.

There were all the men in the family gathered around

her – young and old – some fighting back their tears as the priest spoke about death as if it wasn't new to him. I remember looking back to see my little son fast asleep and thought it best to let him rest.

A part of me is relieved that Zwelami didn't have to experience that moment. Later, it upset me greatly when he asked why I hadn't woken him up. He, at the tender age of eight, had also wanted to say goodbye. To this day he still mentions that he had wanted to see his sister buried.

And now I think that she would have wanted him much closer, because he was also her baby.

―――――•―――――

My life would never be the same again, and it seemed as if my days mattered only to remind me of my loss.

I was hospitalised for another ten days for depression. Before I had left, I'd hidden the plastic bag with Zenani's belongings, but by the time I returned home I was pained to discover that my family had burnt the bag in a traditional ceremony. I was pained, wanting to hold on to it for as long as I could.

Once I was discharged, my drinking only worsened: this time I was downing beer, wine or whiskey with my prescription pills, ignoring that it is disrespectful to drink at a time of mourning. I just didn't want to feel – not if feeling meant having to lose Zenani over and over and over again.

―――――•―――――

My son went to stay with a cousin in Morningside for a short while. After dinner with him one night, I had gone to my grandmother's home in Soweto with my old ex-boyfriend Leo – the one who had introduced me to Ecstasy and magic mushrooms. Our intention was to steal her car, and I'd taken the car keys and had already driven back to the suburbs to buy more alcohol and cocaine when the police stopped us. They threatened to arrest Leo, and we found ourselves withdrawing money at an ATM in order to bribe them. Sitting in my grandmother's car, I looked back at Leo negotiating with the police and my concern was not about the trouble we were in, but how many lines I could snort before they all returned to the car.

Hours later, I was in the parking lot of Malasha, unable to drive and alone after Leo had left me for refusing to have sex with him. I was making small talk with various dealers, who must have been curious about how openly inebriated I was, when Sekoati found me. I was lucky. He'd been sent on my father's orders after my grandmother had reported that I'd disappeared.

On 11 August 2010, I checked myself in Houghton House Addiction Recovery Centre.

I'd had enough and I knew I needed help.

————•◦•————

I spent six weeks on primary care.

As occupants of the house, we addicts had to adhere to clearly stated rules and regulations, which were enforced with the outmost seriousness. If you broke the rules, you were punished accordingly and no one was above Houghton House law – it didn't matter how old you were, your status in society or the colour of your skin. Once you walked into the office, you were only minutes away from being inducted into another whole community.

And of course, I'd had no idea what to expect.

My parents and me shortly after I was born in 1980.

My mother and me as a toddler in the early eighties. I was about two or three years old in this picture.

My stepmother playing with my stepsister, the eldest of their four daughters.

Hanging out at the park.

This picture reminds me so much of my father. He had two or three Beetles at the time.

My grandmother has always made birthdays such a big deal.

This picture of my mother and me kissing is worth its weight in gold!

She was always mommy's ANGEL. I loved her hair. Lala ngoxolo mntanami...

Zenani in a school picture she took at Sacred Heart College.

A school picture. Cutest thing I've ever seen in braces – she got to choose this hairstyle for a change.

Zenani, at the age of five in our Houghton home – most adorable toothless smile!

The first holiday Libra and I took with Zenani and Zwelami to Cape Town – UNFORGETTABLE!

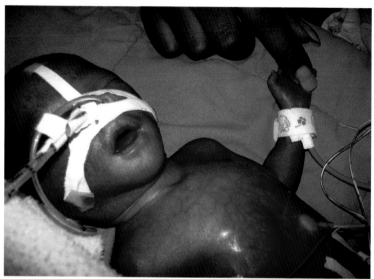

My second son, Zenawe on his hospital bed at Parklane Clinic as I held his hand two days before he passed away. Lala ngoxolo mntanami ...

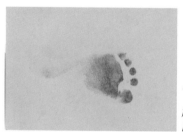

This is Zenawe's footprint just after his birth in 2011, he was such a kicker

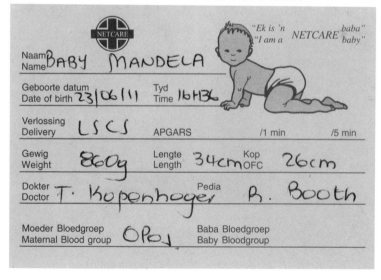

NETCARE

"Ek is 'n NETCARE baba"
"I am a NETCARE baby"

Naam / Name **BABY MANDELA**

Geboorte datum / Date of birth **23/06/11**   Tyd / Time **16H36**

Verlossing / Delivery **LSCS**   APGARS   /1 min   /5 min

Gewig / Weight **860g**   Lengte / Length **34cm**   Kop OFC **26cm**

Dokter / Doctor **T. Kopenhoger**   Pedia **R. Booth**

Moeder Bloedgroep / Maternal Blood group **O Pos**   Baba Bloedgroep / Baby Bloodgroup

My daughter Zenani and me along with family and friends when we celebrated my Zwelami's first birthday in 2003.

Zwelami's school picture taken at Saint Stithians College. He has my lips and gap!

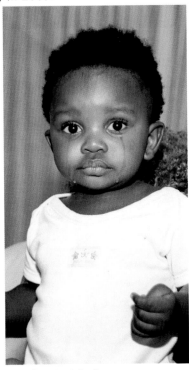

Zwelami with the two most perfect tear tracks rolling down his cheeks.

My school picture taken at Sacred Heart College back in 1991. I loved my German haircut, even if it made me look like a boy!

My cousin and me in a picture we took with Michael Jackson. Reminds me of how shy he was – he reminded me of ME!

If I'd imagined that I'd take some "time out" sitting by the pool reading magazines, I was sorely mistaken. Sure, it was me who had called asking for help. I just hadn't realised the step work that would be involved in undoing years of addiction, or that the process would drive to me escalating levels of emotional hell.

From the beginning, the people at Houghton House saw right through me, but still they showed me acceptance, despite my flaws and demons. When I was asked what help I needed, I responded by saying, "Alcohol and cocaine addiction." I may have tried to brush it off, but at Houghton House I was forced to acknowledge that my addictions didn't stop at substances: I'd had a sexual addiction too, a ghost of the abuse I'd been subjected to as a child. I realised while I was there that my relationship with sex had the same root as my relationship with cocaine: they'd made me feel better about myself.

In primary care we had daily in-house group meetings and attended Narcotics Anonymous and Alcoholic Anonymous meetings throughout the week. In total, I wrote about sixty stories of my experience of addiction, a requirement that followed writing my life story in which I detailed my life before and after drug addiction. We also spent many sessions watching compulsory "consequence movies" – every movie dealt with addiction and its consequences, forcing us to see how our own actions and behaviours had played a role in our addiction. In addition to weekly sessions with my counsellor, there were group meetings and gender meetings ...

Until it all began to get too real.

I started to isolate myself from the group by cleaning. It became almost an automatic response: I'd get up and start dusting or tidying things, and I even remember getting as far as cleaning the windows *outside* the main lecture room.

Removing myself meant I didn't have to deal with the group's dynamics – and I didn't have to deal with me. When I was banned from cleaning, I was forced to speak about myself, and it was something I hated because it came with the responsibility of owning up to the damage that I had caused my family. Most importantly, I had robbed my two children of a mother they deserved.

I kept telling my addiction counsellor that I was in fact there for my children. To prove to myself that I wasn't a failure, I'd try to detail all the times that I'd got them ready for school or helped them with their homework, despite my addiction. But he always stopped me.

"You may have been there physically, but you were not there emotionally for your kids," he said.

I had chosen my addiction over my children, and this reality will haunt me for the rest of my life.

———

It was important for me to have Zwelami come and visit me in the rehabilitation centre. I wanted to see him and spend time with him, but I also needed him to see that I was getting help, and that I wanted to help him. I had lost my only daughter, but he had lost his only sister – how could I be there for him when I had tried everything to numb the pain of my loss?

My family visited me every weekend they were allowed, and I was starting to feel more inspired and determined to make use of the second chance they had given me.

———

After my six weeks in primary care my guidance counsellor

felt it was necessary to proceed with secondary treatment – a programme based on adapting to a new, drug-free lifestyle. That meant having to deal with my daughter's passing, but I felt it was unfair to ask that of me so soon – I already knew that I was not ready. That is how my forty-two days of treatment came to an expected end, and although I was all smiles when my half-brother collected me from the parking area, I had cried all through the night before.

I didn't want to leave any more, and I wondered how they could let me go so soon.

I was scared.

But I was also determined to stay clean. I immediately weaned myself off the antidepressants my psychiatrist had prescribed, since it made no sense to me to have any legal or illegal drug in my system – period. And I decided to do my 90/90: attending ninety meetings in ninety days, and assisting Houghton House patients with transport to Narcotics Anonymous and Alcoholics Anonymous meetings. I also attended what is called "aftercare" on Saturday mornings, where we received continued support at various group meetings after completing our residential treatment.

Although I was adamant to do everything required of me by my addiction counsellor, there were two steps I was just not ready to take. The first was facing my daughter's passing. The second was putting my relationship on the backburner. The idea was that relationships were not ideal while an addict was in recovery – and especially not when the addict used to use drugs and alcohol with his or her lover.

I couldn't have agreed more, however, with the advice that I move out of my mother's Athol home, which had been deemed more threatening than nurturing. I didn't want to go back to my mother's home. Athol was no longer a safe place for me.

Soon after leaving Houghton House I would find myself having to actively avoid the nightly drinking that took place at my mother's house. After attending my NA or AA meetings, I would go out with a friend I'd met in rehab because I didn't want to go home. And when I did go home, I'd head straight to my room.

My mother tried to justify her lack of support.

"The counsellor said we shouldn't have to change *our* lifestyles. You have to because *you* have the problem," she would reiterate.

I didn't want her to change her lifestyle, but only to recognise how it posed a threat to my newfound sobriety and at least try to be more supportive. Knowing that we used to drink together almost every single night, she could have toned it down a little, especially since I had just come out of rehab.

But although there were obstacles, my sobriety was making me happy: I felt like I had a new lease on life, which in turn was making me even more determined to stay clean and sober. My grandmother was making my 90/90 possible by assigning me a driver, who was transporting me in one of her BMWs. Outside of my rehabilitation programme, for a number of months I volunteered at the Orlando Children's Home in Soweto, where I would spend the day with babies and toddlers. And if I wasn't at the Orlando Children's Home, I was at the Princess Alice Adoption Home in Westcliff, where I loved playing with the children.

Feeding these tiny people, changing their diapers and looking after them brought such joy to my heart. Along with my love of my own two children, this experience helped me believe that little children are the closest to God.

When I had checked into Houghton House I had been seeing my Aries, a Zimbabwean-born heartthrob who had been introduced to me by a former friend. We had been using cocaine and alcohol together, but we'd only indulged in our addictions together on Friday nights. He'd been quite strict about that, although I had preferred not having those limits imposed on me. He had soon stopped using, which had upset me greatly at the time, because it felt like he was interfering with my happiness. Back then I couldn't understand why he had wanted to stop, although I came to discover it was for his daughter. Something I should have done for my own children. What had also upset me was that he'd never let me meet his daughter because while I was an addict, he'd found me unfit.

Once I was in the programme at Houghton House, though, I came to see his sobriety as a source of strength. I loved him and I wanted to feel loved by him. I craved him and I wanted him to crave me back. On the weekends that we were allowed visitors, I give him the many letters I'd written to him in the week, and I hated to see him leave. Like putty in a hand, I was weak for this man, unashamedly obsessed with my Aries.

After I'd left Houghton House I'd wanted nothing more than to have a baby with him, which led to at least one hilarious misunderstanding. I remember a conversation I had with him over the phone:

"Baby, I'm five months today!" I said in excitement.

"You're five months *what*?" he asked.

"Today, I'm five months clean and sober!"

Afterwards, I literally rolled on the floor with laughter.

Nevertheless, I was serious about wanting a baby, and he knew how desperate I was. He felt it would be better to wait until we were both ready, though I wanted to convince him otherwise, especially because I was now sober and knew I was part of his "five-year plan".

———•—•———

I met Benzeey, my first Jack Russel, shortly after coming out of rehab, and I adopted him because my Aries had thought a dog would get my mind off trying for a baby. I took my puppy everywhere I went in a cheap Louis Vuitton-lookalike carry bag – it had a hook you could attach to the puppy's collar to secure him while he was in the bag, and two openings on either end for him to pop his head out. I attended quite a few Narcotics Anonymous meetings with Benzeey, a fact that I still find quite hilarious. I developed such a close bond with that puppy, and he is still such a joy to have.

But even my gorgeous puppy couldn't compete with my Aries.

We never saw one another during the week but I always understood that Fridays were for me, Saturdays were for him to take me back home, and Sundays were his to spend with his daughter. For me, saying goodbye every Saturday when he dropped me off would mark the countdown to the next time I could see him. Work prevented him from spending more time with his daughter, and I can appreciate the concern that came with that, but I just couldn't take it when, a few weeks after rehab, he told me that he could only see me every fortnight.

That was rejection if I ever saw it: while I was pining to see more of him, he was wanting to see less of me.

My Aries and I soon broke up, with me in a fit of rage because I wasn't getting my way, although really it was because I felt he was letting go of me. But if I'm really honest, it was because that night he refused for us to have sex. I sent him one last message via cellphone, which terminated our relationship for good.

And true to form, after I'd said my goodbye I moved on to the next. I wholly welcomed rekindling my relationship with Sekoati, primarily out of convenience and because he seemed to give me more attention than my Aries had.

I used to use with him, and my grandmother and mother had reason to be concerned.

Between October and November of 2010, I spent the majority of my free time with Sekoati in the house his uncle rented in Kensington. I couldn't wait to drive over to his place just to see him: we'd spend hours in each other's arms talking about everything. I was falling in love with the man all over again – especially as he demanded more and more of my attention – and if there was ever a time I felt happiest it was in those days when he took care of my heart and my broken soul, although I have come to believe he was still using then.

———•—

By the time Mamma Graça, my grandfather's second wife, had purchased me my first BMW, a white 320d, I was not only out of my mother's house but was reaping the benefits of sobriety. Anyone who cared to listen knew what milestones I'd reached – it was out there on Twitter, Facebook and BBM.

Then, like now, I felt that I had something that I needed to share.

Chapter 16

ON 23 JUNE 2011, AT 4:36 IN the afternoon, I prematurely gave birth to my last born and second son, Zenawe Zibuyile Maiene Mandela, at the Park Lane Clinic. I was only six months into my pregnancy.

I had been suffering from extreme abdominal pains for two days, but I'd been sent home from hospital when the foetal-assessment monitor had ruled out that my son was in any distress. In fact, I'd been in labour for two days before a vaginal scan indicated that there was an infection in my womb and I had to have yet another emergency Caesarean section.

I remember how, surrounded by my family once I had received the dreadful news, I was quickly wheeled into theatre not wasting a single minute. It wasn't until many months later that I watched a video Sekoati showed me of my son's birth, and saw how he had stopped breathing and had to be resuscitated countless times.

After his birth, Zenawe had immediately been taken to ICU, where he was attached with numerous coloured tubes to a machine.

The next two days in hospital were painful physically and emotionally. Sixteen weeks premature, Zenawe was always responsive to touch and although he weighed no more than 860 grams he, like most infants, would grasp my finger in his tiny palm or respond to a touch on his cheek. He would even roll his eyes every now and then. In a personal joke I shared with Sekoati, I nicknamed him Wolverine – I have never seen so much bodily hair on an infant. He was the splitting image of his father, and he had Sekoati's hair too.

I took pictures of him constantly – imagining how I would one day tell him how proud he'd made me by overcoming the life-threatening infection he had developed in my womb and scaring us all half to death.

But every time I hoped he was getting better, he would only get worse. Family and friends placed their hands over Zenawe and said prayers, but despite this, I can't remember how many times the nurses or doctor came into my hospital room to tell me that I needed to get back to ICU because my son had taken a turn. I agreed with Sekoati when he told me he had a feeling that our baby son got worse each time we left him, and so we started spending even more time by his bed, hoping that would help improve his condition. The pain of my stitches and my weak legs weren't enough to stop me from standing by his bed at every opportunity.

But by the time the medical staff announced that my son

was suffering organ failure, it was as if his condition was worsening by the minute and not the hour.

———•———

Two days after his birth, after another emotionally excruciating day, my son suffered more organ failure and he became unresponsive to our touch. My decision to have my newborn baby removed from his life-support machine was not an easy one and it was one I had to make alone, but I could no longer watch him fight to his own detriment.

The infection in my womb had found its way to my baby's body before it had reached mine, and in a way I feel he saved my life. Had I not gone into labour, we would not have known the extent of the infection, although numerous subsequent tests conducted to uncover the cause of the infection have proved futile.

Still, there is not a day that goes by where I am not left weakened by the thought that I could perhaps have done something differently to save his life.

When he finally arrived, Sekoati and I called my family, who had been coming in shifts to support and pray with us, to tell them that I had made the decision to release him from life support. In just moments I had my brothers, my mother and Sekoati with me in a room the medical staff had given us to use. My family all got their turn to say their goodbyes to him.

His father and I had said we would do whatever it took to take care of Zenawe, but we had never considered that he wouldn't be coming home with us. Leaving him behind, all alone, was never a reality until he'd taken his final breath in my arms.

———•———

In the hours that followed, one of the nurses came to give me a massage. As I undressed I noticed how full my breasts were, and it tore me up as I remembered how the nurses had come to collect my breast milk for Zenawe. I later learnt that my son had been unable to feed on my breast milk. I cried for what felt like forever each time I felt the let-down reflex, or when my breasts became engorged with Zenawe's milk. Soon after, my gynaecologist prescribed tablets to assist with drying up the milk.

I wish I had been given the opportunity to bathe Zenani as I did Zenawe on the day before his burial. And the experience was totally unlike when I had bathed my late step-sister Kefuoe a day before her burial, which had left me traumatised.

When I walked into the mortuary with my mother and Zenawe's paternal grandmother, there he was, my little soldier lying there. I looked at him for a long time and noticed the calmness in his face.

He was smiling, which I believe made it easier for me to give him his bath before I dressed him up and covered him in his blankets.

—•—

Although every day is a constant, incomprehensible reminder of the agony and anger I still feel, I realise that God loved me so much that he blessed Zwelami and me with two angels: Zenani and Zenawe.

He shared them with us briefly, just as we are now sharing them with Him.

Chapter 17

ALTHOUGH I HAD BEEN FRIENDS WITH Sekoati for many years before venturing into a romantic relationship with him, towards the end of our relationship it became obvious that a future together was non-existent. After the initial bliss, our relationship had become turbulent, and I'd felt that he'd never really been there for me as I had thought. Although it shouldn't have surprised me, I was often at my loneliest when I was with him.

I also hesitated in believing that he was willing to get – and stay – clean. It became clear to both of us that on my path to sobriety I could no longer affiliate myself with anyone who posed a threat to my recovery.

I had to part ways with him in order to protect myself.

With help from my Aunt Zenani and my grandmother, in the months following my time at rehab, I had finally moved into my own place in Fourways. My aunt had tasked herself with purchasing crockery and cutlery, and I was feeling so much better for having taken this step towards independence.

I had allowed Sekoati into my new home on the condition that he would remain clean. But, soon after I'd conceived Zenawe, I'd found marijuana residue in the Chrysler which my grandmother had loaned me, and which I'd allowed him to use. I'd found used-up marijuana joints in my garden and, when I was doing his laundry, I found pieces of plastic which traces of heroin in the pockets of his pants, which he claimed had been worn by his friends.

Each time I gave him the opportunity to confess or come clean.

Over the next few months I never believed his lies, but I allowed it to continue, though I was in no way protecting my son, Zwelami, as I should have. I believe that Sekoati chose his drug over me, and at my expense, and it became unbearable as I realised that I was becoming an enabler.

As an addict myself, I am quite aware of the ability of your addiction to render you completely helpless. An addict will do whatever it takes to ensure access to their drug of choice, and at any expense. I have never been able to forgive Sekoati for leaving me at the hospital when our little Zenawe was fighting for his life, or for all those days I spent at home alone after his passing, when we should have been mourning our loss together.

We have a centuries-old tradition in our family: ten days after a child's birth, their umbilical cord is buried in the soil in an area of our grandmother's choosing. At my home in

Soweto, when the time came for us to partake in this family custom, Sekoati was nowhere to be found.

That was the final straw. When he finally arrived – after the ceremony had finished – I grabbed my car keys from him and, still in pain from the Caesarean, I drove myself home. Hurt and angry, I made a conscious decision to free myself from him since he was clearly not willing to get and stay clean. After terminating my relationship with Sekoati on that day, the next time I saw him was only a month or two later at my grandmother's home in Soweto, when we performed a ritual signifying the end of our mourning.

A few days after that, he called me and asked me to come to see him.

I guess in some way I wanted to believe that he'd made a change for the better, so I was taken aback to find him suffering from withdrawal symptoms in the room of a bed and breakfast, without a penny to his name. He was my son's father, and there was no way I could walk away from that situation knowing I could have helped. I invited him back into my home so that I could at least make his unpleasant withdrawal symptoms more bearable, and provide the emotional support he would no doubt need. I told him I would help him for however long it took, on the condition that he remained clean. But being together was no longer something I wanted, and I never intended for us to find a way back to each other.

In fact, it was during this time that I had felt the need to inform him of a relationship I had developed with someone else. Although that relationship soon came to an abrupt end when the man moved countries for his job, at the time I wanted at least to give it a chance. I told Sekoati about it one afternoon as we were sitting outside on my patio smoking a cigarette together, because I didn't want him to find out about my new relationship from anyone else. I was in the habit of discussing my relationships openly, even on social networks.

A few days later, he texted my mother to tell her that I had moved on, but he hadn't taken it very well.

And then there was more lying and more using on his part. Having come so far, I started to realise that in inviting Sekoati into my home, I had just taken a huge step backwards. I had opened the door to more hurt and more deceit. Yet again, I had put someone else's priorities ahead of my own, and ahead of Zwelami's.

Nine days after he'd moved in, the security at my gate assisted him with his belongings, which I left outside my front door for him to collect.

I expected him to be angry and hurt – we were good at making each other feel that way – but I never expected the disrespect and pain that he caused me when he posted insulting messages about my family and me on Facebook, and which were brought to my attention by a mutual friend. Although he later removed them, the damage had already been done. To add insult to injury, he continued to shame my family and me with untruths that he shared with various publications.

I had failed my family by being unable to protect them as they had protected me. I attempted to clear my name, but I soon realised that the journalist I had approached in my defence was more interested in selling the story than assisting me with setting the record straight. Trying to save my son's father was sinking me, and it was time to start saving myself.

My son and my family deserved to experience a better

Zoleka – a Zoleka who was willing to better herself and her loved ones by staying clean, sober and independent.

———•◦•———

After giving birth to Zenawe I had weighed eighty-four kilograms and so once I had broken it off with Sekoati I focused my attention on losing weight. I changed my diet and worked out every single day. I'd start off with a morning jog, during which I would drop Zwelami off at school, and then I'd work out to a Zumba DVD I'd bought.

Within nine months I had dropped eighteen kilograms and had taken up boxing, which I did two to three times every week for three months. For the first time in ages, I looked and felt good about myself.

PART II

The greatest glory of living lies not in never falling,
but in rising every time we fall.

~ Nelson Rolihlahla Mandela

Chapter 18

I WAS RAISED BY SUCH STRONG women: my grandmother, my Aunt Zenani and my mother.

My Aunt Zenani has always been a mother to me in every sense of the word. Like my grandmother, her presence is so deeply imbedded in my life that it would be difficult to describe my own strength without recognising that so much of it comes from her. Along with my grandmother, she has held my hand through my most difficult moments, despite the many times I have let go from her grip. Her support and encouragement have remained unwavering. She is a phenomenal woman, and what really strikes me is how she never needs to seek the approval of others to confirm who she already is.

Many years ago, at a prayer group held at my mother's house, the members of the group and some of my cousins were individually tasked to write something about our relationship with God. I wrote a poem. At that particular stage in my life I was very conflicted: my relationship with God had come to an impasse and I generally found it easier to shift blame than to begin unpacking my own baggage. Over the years it had become almost impossible for me to recognise my own walk.

It was my Aunt Zenani who steered me in the direction of understanding and forgiveness, and of faith in God.

———

I remember making my way with my family to the scene of Zenani's accident to place flowers where she'd taken her last breath. As soon as my car door opened I noticed her black-and-white sock lying on the pavement. I knew it was hers instantly, and I remember grabbing it and dusting it off before clinging to it for the longest time. As a family, we'd gone to perform a traditional ceremony whereby one's spirit is ushered from where the body took its last breath, so that it can find its way back home.

I would battle with the images I saw that morning: my daughter's blood all over the road barrier. To this day I can't bring myself to travel anywhere near there. I attended the trial and I was gutted to see, along with the entire court room, a display with the route that marked the end of my daughter's life. Every time we listened to the proceedings in court I would ask myself how it was possible that we were all gathered in that room two years after Zenani's passing. And why was this man pleading not guilty? He had sat on my bed with me there in my grandmother's home in Soweto and confessed that he had been drunk when he drove her. How could he now be defended?

I took her black-and-white sock and placed it in a new Bible my aunt had bought me. It made sense to me to put it between those pages, because I wanted to believe that she was now with Him.

For months I could not bring myself to visit Zenani's final resting place. During that time, my Aunt Zenani went every single weekend, taking flowers, which she placed in the flower pots she'd brought, tidying up and watering the grave and scattering pink rose petals all over it. For me, the idea that Zenani might be alone nearly drove me insane with pain. How could I leave her there in the cemetery?

For a very long time I felt that wherever she was she was feeling cold, and no matter how many times my aunt reminded me that we had buried her with a huge winter blanket, I don't think anyone understood what I meant. Zenani was cold and needed me to be with her and to keep her warm. I wanted to die so I could be with my baby, to hold her and keep her warm, but how could we possibly arrive at the same place after everything I had done and the person I had become over the years?

Chapter 19

I MET ANOTHER SOURCE OF great strength in the summer of early 2012. His arrival into my life was unexpected, but the timing couldn't have been more perfect – I never knew then how much I was going to come to depend on him.

It was January and I had just moved into a new place in another Fourways complex, which I had chosen specifically because it was in walking distance of where Zenani and Zenawe have been laid to rest. Zwelami wasn't at home because it was school holidays and he was visiting his cousin in Parkmore, so I'd taken a drive to Fourways Mall to buy that elusive pair of perfect fitting jeans. I was still in the process of losing weight, and I had got used to hiding my body underneath maxi dresses – I was seldom comfortable enough about my body to wear jeans, which usually ended up unworn at the bottom of my closet.

I'd just walked into Edgars, where I was browsing, when I heard someone greet me. Here was this handsome and very young man – dark skinned, with a little afro, an ungroomed beard and a goatee, who couldn't possibly be more than a year or two into varsity. He asked me what I was shopping for and, thinking that he worked there, I told him I was wanting to buy some jeans. He pointed to the dark blue jeans I'd just been looking at and asked me to come out the change room and show him once I had tried them on.

Of course I refused, but when I realised that he wasn't actually selling the jeans I was pretty amused – who was this guy following me around the store? I tried on the jeans, which I didn't actually like, but before I could leave he had asked for my number. I was smiling as I walked away in the direction of the car park – at his request, I'd spontaneously given him my number by calling his cell and letting it ring once, which felt like the silliest thing to do. But I liked how confident and charming he'd seemed, not to mention persistent!

His name was Thierry.

As I started thinking about it, though, my feelings started to change. I was probably a good eight years older than him after all, so why had he felt he had any business talking to me in the first place? In fact, the more I thought about it, the more I started to think how rude it was.

And then he didn't end up calling me when he said he would – and that really irked me.

The next day I called him to give him a piece of my mind. Hours later we were still on the phone, talking about anything and everything. I found him so easy to talk to – and that he was merely three years my junior, which somehow I didn't mind so much, despite having always preferred older men.

That call was the first of many, and we haven't stopped talking since.

We spent our first night together at my complex in Craigavon. That night the entire complex suffered a power cut. In the darkness of the lounge, I found and lit all the candles I had. At that point in my life I'd had no intention of finding a new relationship – either with him or anyone else – but as we sat on my black leather couch and talked by candlelight, he put his head in my lap and my fingers found their way from the base of his neck to the tip of his head, and I hoped that the electricity wouldn't come back on at all. The universe had created an ambience.

Because in that particular moment with that particular man, I was in the one place in the world that I wanted to be.

Just right there.

Meeting Thierry was a huge light in my life, and I always say that he was "unexpectedly on time".

We started dining out four or five times a week, and spent a lot of time together. The closer we got, the more reasons we found to stay together. If the heart had a mind of its own, mine would spend its days thinking about him.

It was the simple things that we did so well. I remember sitting at a hair salon, and he was waiting for me, sitting opposite my chair. I was in a panic at how long it was taking for the hairdresser to finish, and I sent him an SMS apologising.

His response? "Take your time, baby ... Watching you makes me happy." He always made me weak at the knees, even with the smallest effort.

He always saved the day, my Congolese-born knight in shining armour who taught me the importance of prayer and who still prays with me to this day.

I say that Thierry was "unexpectedly on time" because there was something I had been in denial about since the previous year. Something that was to take quite a while for me to deal with.

It couldn't have been more than a month or two after I'd lost my son Zenawe that I'd noticed an abnormality in my left breast.

My first thought was that it must have been a side effect from the medication to dry up my breast milk. Months had passed though, and as they did, the growth in my breast became more defined, until I could feel it distinctly, just behind my nipple.

It was a Sunday in March when I finally brought up the topic with my Aunt Zenani. We were visiting Zenani and Zenawe, as we do every Sunday, together with my grandmother, Zwelami and now Thierry, and afterwards I opened up to my aunt about the abnormality that was now becoming a concern: my lump had become two lumps, and the worry had doubled.

She gave me a number to call to set up an appointment at a radiology practice in Illovo.

—•—

On the day of my scheduled appointment, I was consumed with worry.

I was quite familiar with the area to which I was headed, as my family and I frequented a restaurant nearby, and when I was in the lift I noticed that the practice was almost directly on top of the restaurant – but really I was just trying to distract myself.

Inside the waiting room there were two women sitting behind a large desk to my right, and on my left were several chairs surrounding a coffee table with magazines, where a few older women sat waiting their turn, not saying a word to each other. I was given a client form to fill in and I went to sit with the other women; when I was done, I too grabbed a magazine. I remember stealing a few stares and wondering why each of them were there, and I was struck by the thought that I was the youngest of the women by far.

When, finally, it was my turn, a nurse called me to the door as she had done with all the other women, and I was shown to a cubicle down the passage. I was told to remove everything from the waist up and to make use of an orange hospital gown that was hanging there. Someone else's clothes were still hanging in the cubicle, but as we hadn't been assigned our own cubicles, I went ahead and got undressed.

Wearing the orange hospital gown, I kept my handbag with me and found an empty seat in a different room that was indicated to me, with more women in orange hospital gowns, and yet more magazines.

When the nurse came once more for me, I was led to a single room where I was asked to lie down on the bed for an examination. I wondered how many women had lain on the same bed – none of us knowing what to expect, and all of us wanting for this all to be over. I lay with my breasts fully exposed to the female doctor and nurse as I was asked to lift one or both of my hands over my head, or to place them at my sides. The doctor spoke to me throughout the exam, asking questions, leaving little of the surface of my breasts untouched. It was not unlike the breast exams I'd had during the checkups I'd gone to with all my pregnancies.

Then I was taken into another room where I was told how to position myself on the machine so they could conduct a mammogram. I remember how bright the room was, and how it felt as if the machine was swallowing up my breast each time the female technician told me to reposition myself. There was pressure as the machine squeezed my breast from both the top and the bottom, me standing the entire time, until the technician was satisfied with her adjustments. Sometimes I had to hold my breath and keep still. For a moment I felt as if my breast was going to burst from the pressure – I didn't know then that the reason it's done like this is to spread out the breast tissue for the X-ray. But I did what I was told, hoping that the sooner I followed the instructions the quicker I would be out of there.

Until, finally, I was.

I hadn't been much of a smoker at that point, and there was hardly a packet of cigarettes to my name, but on my way home from the centre I was already planning a cigarette. That afternoon I sat on the step outside my kitchen door, where it didn't feel as if I was being watched by my neighbours, who otherwise would have had full view of what I was doing. If I was going to smoke, I did not want to be seen.

I was very anxious during the interminable wait for my results from the doctors' rooms. I was stressed and I needed a distraction. Because alcohol and drugs were not an option, I took to smoking cigarettes again. Although I did not openly smoke in front of Zwelami, he always seemed to know when I had.

"Mom, are you stressed? Because you say you smoke when you are stressed," he'd say.

A couple of days after my appointment the doctor asked me to return. At my second consultation I was told that the mammogram had indeed shown an abnormality in my left breast. I was going to need a breast biopsy so that a sample of the mass located in my breast could be sent to a laboratory for further investigation.

So it was confirmed: there was something to be worried about. I can't say that I was in full panic mode or anything like that, but I remember having to psych myself up for what would come next.

When I was also told about the procedure of the breast biopsy, or rather a core needle biopsy, it sounded very much like surgery, and I thought it would mean I'd need to make another appointment. I was surprised when the doctor said she would perform the biopsy right there and then, in the consulting room.

But that was nothing compared to the incredible shock of pain I felt during the biopsy, despite the local anaesthetic – I could still feel the needle pushing right through the skin of my breast and ripping into the lump, before being pulled quickly out. And as if that wasn't enough, the doctor told me she would need to do this at least several times more. It all happened while I was awake, and how I wished they could have put me to sleep before tearing into my diseased breast. I just really wanted to cry, and I was so sad I had gone to the appointment alone.

After samples of my breast tissue had been extracted several times, there was some bleeding. The procedure had taken longer than I had expected, and all the way through I'd wanted to yell and tell the doctor to stop. I remember that when she was finally finished, and I was still lying on the bed in the consultation room, I turned my head to her and asked whether she thought I had cancer.

Although I had toyed with the idea of the lump being caused by the medication to dry up my breast milk, I'd had a feeling all along that it was cancerous. I was aware that the lump had mutated, and my entire left breast felt completely different to my right. Touching it felt like I had a million tiny balls inside, in addition to those two lumps that seemed to be the source of all the pain.

Why did she pause when I asked her? That is never a good sign, is it?

I think I rephrased the question a second time and asked whether we had something to worry about. Her words were that there was something quite concerning, although she was not able to confirm at that stage that it was cancer. But it no longer mattered what she replied, because that small pause had said it all – that, and the look on her face. It looked like she was breaking the news to her own daughter.

She was worried and I was officially in Big Trouble.

I was in pain as I got out of my orange hospital gown and changed back into my clothes. At reception I settled my bill before opening the door leading outside, where I was met by a cold wind that brought with it heavy rain.

I got into my car, which was parked opposite the centre, and I couldn't drive.

I was scared. I didn't know what to do, or what to think. And I was alone.

It took close to an hour for me to compose myself. I think the trauma of the breast biopsy and the possibility that I may have cancer only actually hit me once I'd got into my car. I remember watching the rain drops running down my car window at the same time as tears were falling down my cheeks.

The first person I called was my Aunt Zenani. When I couldn't get a hold of her, I called my grandmother, who answered her phone almost immediately.

"Ma, I think I have cancer." I was crying so much that she could barely make out what I was saying.

"Where are you, darling? I'm coming right now."

I probably could have handled the situation better than I did, because I only made her worry more. I had to tell her that I would be okay just so she wouldn't get too stressed about it. By the time my Aunt Zenani had called me back, my grandmother had already spoken to the doctor, and I was still sitting completely immobilised in my car. At that point, in my head, I thought I had just received a death sentence.

"Darling, I've spoken to the doctor. Don't worry – you have an aunt who has gone through the same thing." My grandmother's niece had had breast cancer – and for me, what she was saying just served as yet another confirmation.

I do not know what words were exchanged between my grandmother and the doctor, but I got the feeling that she knew something that I didn't. She later told me that the doctor had mentioned that they encourage patients not to come for mammograms alone because they know it is important for people to have support. Knowing the family I came from, the doctor had been quite surprised that I'd been alone at both appointments. For my part, I'd been worried, but not to the point that I'd felt I needed my grandmother, my Aunt Zenani or Thierry there.

How wrong I had been.

Chapter 20

I will remain indebted to my grandmother for as long as there is life in me. Her ability to see the strength in me always leaves me galvanised and in "warrior mode", and it has been this way not just on my journey with breast cancer, but with the loss of my two angels in Heaven, as well as my path to sobriety. I know now more than I did growing up just how genuinely invested she is in having me succeed in all aspects of my life.

It was this strength that I was going to need in the coming months, as I had drawn on it in the past.

——◆——

My Aunt Zenani recommended that we get a second opinion, and so we made an appointment with Dr Carol-Ann Benn, a specialist surgeon and breast-disease specialist at the Netcare Breast Care Centre of Excellence at the Milpark Hospital. In the days leading up to it, I tried to smoke my worry away on the end of a dying Marlboro Light, Peter Stuyvesant Blue or Camel Light. As much as I didn't want to participate in what was happening, the uncertainty around my diagnosis was killing me.

On 15 March 2012, a few days after the initial breast biopsy, I met Dr Benn.

I consider my first consultation with Dr Benn as that of my official breast cancer diagnosis. It wasn't until she had accessed the results of my breast biopsy that I knew for sure that the tests had shown I had ductal cancer in one breast. After seeing the ease with which Dr Benn was able to access my medical file, I kept wondering why the previous doctor hadn't told me sooner. Why hadn't she alerted me after the medical exam, the breast biopsy or when she'd had confirmation of the tests? I'd probably smoked my lungs black because I'd just wanted to know.

But then the real question hit me: "Am I going to die?"

My father's sister, my aunt Violet Seakamela, had had breast cancer and had undergone chemotherapy after the mastectomy of one breast. After winning her initial battle, the cancer had returned. She'd refused treatment the second time round and succumbed to her breast cancer in November 1992 at the age of thirty-two – the very same age I was at the time of my diagnosis. I don't remember my aunt being sick or in pain, and I don't remember watching her slowly slip through our fingers. I don't recall the days leading up to her passing, or the things she loved to say and do.

All I recall is my father saying that I had beautiful hands – just like my aunt Violet.

I say that I wanted to know but, walking into Dr Benn's consulting room, if I'd been told that I had breast cancer, I would have asked for a refund on my movie ticket.

I felt I was in a horror film, and I was finding it impossible to even comprehend. I'd had Zenani and Zenawe taken from me, and now there was the sudden reality that I may never again breastfeed or carry another pregnancy. I had lost two babies and now I was losing even the possibility of finding that love again. I explained to Dr Benn that I had breastfed Zenani and Zwelami for a solid two years each – so how could I be denied that right in the future?

Why is all this happening? I asked myself.

"There is nothing you did to cause this – it's in your genes," Dr Benn said as I sat across from her, weeping.

But I battled to understand that no matter what I'd done, or how I'd done it, I would always have ended up getting cancer. It had always had a hold on me, and it felt like an old boyfriend seeking revenge. I started bargaining: If I can never breastfeed again, please God let me be able to carry my babies in my own womb.

Sitting there at the appointment, as I battled with what it all meant, I was told that time was of the essence. To understand what we were dealing with, I would need to have a sentinel lymph node biopsy on my left breast, which would be performed in hospital after a scheduled breast MRI (Magnetic Resonance Imaging).

On the same day at the Breast Care Centre, we also met with Dr Karen Appelbaum, the clinical psychologist just doors away from Dr Benn – and the resident "breast psychologist". My breast cancer diagnosis had left me with a range of emotions, and I was struggling to digest everything the doctors had told me. My inability to share these emotions with Dr Appelbaum during our first and only consultation had a lot to do with the difficulty I was having absorbing it all.

At that point I couldn't even comprehend the types of decisions I was going to have to make, and the whole thing felt rushed.

Just two weeks later I was admitted to Milpark Hospital under a pseudo name.

After completing the admission paperwork, the nurse talked me through the process of my overnight stay in the hospital. My family arrived in their numbers to show their unconditional support, but I was alone when I was taken to the room where the MRI would be performed.

The doctor and mammographer explained the procedure.

I was asked to sit up as they injected a blue liquid called a radioisotope dye into the left side of my breast – this, it was explained, would provide them with sentinel node mapping. The dye flows through the lymph system to the exact location of the sentinel lymph nodes, colouring them blue, and providing a much clearer view of any cysts, enlarged ducts, enlarged lymph nodes, breast abnormalities and so forth. I was then asked to lie face down onto a moveable padded table, ensuring that my breasts fitted into hollow depressions that were connected to the MRI machine. The table slid into the actual machine, which looked like a tunnel, and the whole test would take about an hour.

I was so anxious. I'd never been on anything like this before. My Aunt Zenani had advised me to bring along my earphones, which I had forgotten, and I had to endure the mechanical sound of the machine as the minutes ticked slowly by. I found myself dozing off, only to be woken up by the voice of the nurse who could communicate with me through speakers. She asked if I was okay, which I found most comforting.

And then for the next ordeal. Finally in surgery for the sentinel lymph node biopsy, I had several lymph nodes surgically extracted through an incision on my left armpit – these are the first nodes that the cancer would spread to. If there is no cancer in these nodes, then chances are that the other nodes have not been affected and can be left alone.

The procedure took another hour.

I spent the night in hospital and after being discharged I was sent home with a drainage system and a document to record the amount of blood or fluid I was draining every day. I also received a discharge advice sheet, which would assist me in caring for my wound and preventing infection.

Sitting on my couch in my lounge with my mother and grandmother a few hours later, though, my discomfort had grown into unbearable pain. The throbbing in my left armpit made lifting my arm far too painful.

Before the surgery, the lumps in my left breast had felt like two cashew nuts. In the week after my breast biopsy they felt like they had merged into one mass – and instead of two cashew nuts, my entire breast felt like it was stuffed with cement the size of a tennis ball. It was very swollen and painful to touch.

I knew that I would have to return to hospital a week later in order to have the surgical drain removed – but, I was told, only if I had expelled enough liquid. I would need to measure the amount of liquid that was drained every day and record it in a table on a pamphlet I'd received. I hated seeing the blood and other fluid slowly making its way down the plastic tube, so I would tap it with my fingernails to help it travel to where I'd placed the bottle on the floor. When I needed to move around, I put the bottle in a wooden carrier with two handles.

My mother came with me on the day I was to have it removed, and I walked into the ward carrying the drainage system and wearing high heels. I must have looked silly to the now-familiar faces of the nurses, but I felt incredibly good about leaving the drainage system behind, and I was excited about not having to carry it with me everywhere.

I hadn't realised until then that the tube for the drainage system came from the same incision that they'd used to remove my nodes, and that it was secured to my body with stitches. I was told to take a deep breath as they took it out … and the excruciating pain from the tube detaching itself from my armpit was unexpected and aggressive. I closed my eyes as I felt the nurse struggle to removing the last stitch, feeling like a piece of my armpit was being pulled out along with the tube.

Before being sent home once again to await my biopsy results, I was told not to drive or shower until my wound had healed.

A week later I consulted with Dr Benn so that she could relate the findings of the biopsy. My family, thank goodness, were there with me, because it was on this day that I would learn that I not only had two tumours, but that I also had cancerous cells and cysts all over my left breast. Before the Left Sentinel Biopsy the ultrasound had revealed that there was no cancer in my glands; now it had spread to the glands and was trying to spread further. Recovery would require not only a mastectomy, but chemotherapy.

I was broken.

Dr Benn recommended a course of treatment, but I was so wounded and angry that I left the Breast Care Centre of Excellence with no intention of returning. It would be a little over three months before I set foot there again.

Chapter 21

I HAD NEVER REALLY HAD A healthy attitude of responsibility towards my breasts – I'm not sure many of us do. I'd never really taken the importance of breast self-examinations seriously, because I'd felt my breasts should be reserved strictly for my children, and the only others to touch them should be doctors.

Now, memories about my breasts came flooding back.

I remember being a young teenager when we still lived in Observatory: it was after school, and four friends and I were in my room changing out of our yellow Sacred Heart College tunics and getting into our bathing costumes for a dip in the pool. One of my friends was rating who had the biggest breasts, and it bothered me that I only ranked at number three. I remember how perky my breasts were at that age. After the others had gone downstairs, I stood bare breasted in front of the mirror – as I did so many times after that day – wondering what I would look like when they were bigger.

And then there was the afternoon in high school, after I'd given birth to Zenani. I was sitting in my Biology class upstairs at Damelin Eden College and I hadn't noticed that my tight-fitting yellow top was wet until one of my classmates pointed at my breasts. When I looked down my breasts were twice their normal size. I'd been told that when you felt the let-down reflex, it meant that your baby was ready for their feed. I probably hadn't expressed enough milk before leaving the house for my standard-nine classes. In my mind, I could just see Zenani crying because it was time for me to get home and feed her.

When I had stopped breastfeeding Zenani, my breasts were terribly engorged and it looked like I was hiding lumpy cottage cheese underneath my skin. It got extremely uncomfortable and in desperation I recall having to ask my Capricorn to suck on my breasts – that alleviated the pain almost immediately, although it defeated the whole purpose of stopping the milk production.

But they were there: memories about the breasts that I felt had now failed me.

Chapter 22

AFTER THE BIOPSY, DAYS BECAME weeks, and weeks became months, and I did absolutely everything I could to distract myself from the reality of my situation. For a little while I avoided any conversation about my diagnosis, and I think it was pretty clear to my family that I had chosen not to receive treatment for my cancer.

In my defence, I felt I would much rather live the duration of my life to the fullest than spend it fighting a losing battle with cancer. The photos that Dr Benn had showed me of women who had left their breast cancer untreated weren't enough to change my mind, and neither were the stories of the horrendous smell that exudes from untreated breast tissue and the horrific disfigurement of the diseased breasts.

But I battled with this decision I was making. I was absolutely miserable, and I spent three months crying endless tears, and questioning God and life itself.

I cried at any depiction of cancer in any movie – and, for some reason, every other movie I now saw seemed to be about someone battling cancer, just as every other topic on the radio was about the same thing. I couldn't get away from it – wherever I was, and whatever I was doing or saying, I had it right there with me. Cancer wasn't going anywhere and I had become a statistic.

I felt I had been let down by my body.

———•——

I strongly believe that Thierry came into my life because he had a specific role to play. Even from the very beginning of our relationship, after I'd disclosed my diagnosis to him, he hadn't treated me any differently. The cancer hadn't changed a thing. Whether we disagreed or made up, he swept me off my feet and caught me whenever I felt I was losing my balance.

When I had been admitted to hospital for my biopsy, he had spent the night in hospital with me, and even in my intoxicated state I knew he was standing at my hospital bed feeding me. It was so reassuring to open my eyes and know that he was right there in the room with me and that he hadn't left, despite how tired he was or how uncomfortable the night spent on the blue hospital couch must have been. He knew of my weakness for the peppermint caramel sundae from Woolworths and I was so warmed when he bought one to put in the mini fridge in my hospital room, just in case I fancied some later. Over and over he had proved himself to be so thoughtful and selfless. With Thierry it was real, and there was nothing about him that pitied me. I loved his maturity, and through it all being with him had become my all-time happy place.

Of course, coming at a time like this, there were also challenges in our union. For one, we started to argue about my refusal to get treatment – but no matter how upset he got with me, and no matter what he said, I felt that it was my own decision to make and not his. I think Thierry may have even called me selfish a few times, and it was selfish – but I hadn't completely processed it all. My grandmother and Aunt Zenani were also pleading with me to reconsider my decision – if not for treatment, then at least to get a third opinion if I was not yet satisfied. On this subject, no one was getting through to me.

I honestly believe that God sent Thierry to me because of my inability to ask for help.

Over three months, I became depressed, helpless and angry – all at the same time.

"Zoleka, you have been through far worse. You can overcome this too," I was told.

Yes, I had been through far worse, but the loss and suffering I had already experienced in my life didn't make this any easier to deal with.

And I wondered about Zenani, and how she would have dealt with my diagnosis. She and I were always a mess for each other. If she was away and I called, we'd both end up crying on opposite ends of the telephone. Someone once said that she thought my cancer was caused by all the heartache and loss I had endured after my daughter lost her life. It had me thinking – if I had to recognise my most difficult feelings, then guilt would be one of them.

For all those times when Zenani asked me not to leave, when I should have stayed at home with her.

For when I should have let her sleep in the mornings just a few minutes more, because I know how much she loved that, how difficult she found waking up.

I should have let her raid my closet for all the shoes and clothes she loved, instead of shouting at her for wearing them without my permission.

To the child who loved and adored me, I should have been an amazing mother. But I wasn't.

I should have shielded her from any harm, because she had a right to my protection.

She didn't deserve a mother like me.

If I am brutally honest, I could say that from the time of my daughter's passing, my only plea to God had been to allow me the opportunity to be the type of mother she deserved – in this life or the next. I wanted to be the one who'd been with her in her time of need, even if it meant my own life had to be taken.

Losing my life to cancer would mean that I no longer had to deal with my two children's passing, and I sincerely hoped it would mean a life with them.

———•———

I am so ashamed that I had to hear from my loved ones that it was my son Zwelami that I should have been thinking of.

It was while I was in the space of denial that I came across a documentary on M-Net about the life of a woman with breast cancer. Normally any movie or show relating to cancer had me switching channels in tears, because suddenly everything was a reminder of how diseased I felt I was. The main focus of this documentary was a charity banquet the woman was hosting to assist those cancer patients who didn't qualify for financial aid. In doing so, she developed a close friendship with a woman she had come to admire for her strength and determination to fight her cancer. In the end, her friend lost her battle shortly after receiving treatment that left her father financially ruined while mourning the death of his daughter.

I was watching the documentary lying in the comfort of my bed, and I realised how fortunate I really was – not only because my cancer was at an early stage, but also because it was treatable. I saw how irresponsibly and selfishly I had been behaving: here I was with the opportunity to receive the best medical treatment in the country, and I was choosing to rather have the disease swallow me up from the inside because that decision was easier.

Dr Benn had mentioned that smaller cancers could be more aggressive than bigger ones, and even though my cancer was known to be slow growing, it was just a matter of time before it made its way from the inside of my left breast to the rest of my body. If I was going to fight this battle, I would need to admit to myself that the cancer was, in fact, my reality.

I called my grandmother in tears, and although she couldn't make out what I was saying, she got the gist of it: I was going to receive treatment, if not for myself, then for my family. For Zwelami, I would fight the cancer.

I had finally made the decision to save my life.

——◆——

Having made that decision, I still wasn't quite ready to take that step, and there were still a few issues I had to resolve. For one, before I called Dr Benn to inform her of my decision I knew I had to have a conversation with my son.

Back in April, Dr Benn had been kind enough to offer

to speak to Zwelami with me about my diagnosis so that we could answer his questions together. But it felt more comfortable to speak to him at home. In private, the way I felt it needed to be, the first thing he asked me was, "Mom, are you going to die?"

A part of me still wanted to die.

Zwelami has had to grow up far too quickly – I have been reminded by my grandmother on numerous occasions that I forget he is just a child. As much as his first question got to the heart of the matter, he wasn't really able to open up about his other feelings about my cancer. Perhaps he would have had more to say if he were talking to Zenani, because I know how close they were. He never wants to talk about his sister, and when he occasionally does, I am always relieved that he is at least communicating. I've also come to realise that just because he is not crying or saying anything, it does not mean that he is not feeling something that needs to be addressed.

I realise now, too, that my son's feelings about my cancer were determined by my own attitude towards it. Understandably, he'd interpreted my denial as fear. I now saw that the best thing I could do for him was to be honest about my disease and make him part of the process. I decided to always remind him that we could talk about anything, any time, including the birds and the bees.

I knew he would feel his own fear and a world of emotions, and he might develop other insecurities, but I was determined that whenever he was at home or when we were together, everything would be Normal, with a capital N.

———◆———

I was in a relatively good space on the weekend in early June when, en route to my house one weekend, I saw a notice advertising the sale of several Jack Russell puppies in the neighbourhood. I immediately took down the number and called. That evening I convinced Thierry that it would be a great idea to get a puppy that we could raise together as a family, and the next day, Zwelami, Thierry and I brought home Thizo, an eight-week-old pup, to join our other furry son, Benzeey. "Thizo" is a combination of our names – a name which Thierry would later register under for the Nike We Run Jozi run. The name appeared on his shirt in the race, which I thought was the cutest thing, especially when his fellow runners unknowingly called him Thizo.

It was also later that month I had a tattoo done – my tenth – as a reminder to my future self of the time that I survived cancer. It is composed of the date of my diagnosis – "March 2012" – with the inscription "Survivor" right above it, and I decided to place it just below my left breast, on my ribs, so that it would remain when my breasts were gone.

Chapter 23

DURING THE THREE MONTHS OF my denial, an uncle of mine had passed away just days after his birthday. And my grandmother had been hospitalised at Milpark for almost a week.

I assume that Dr Benn had heard about my grandmother while she was on her rounds, because she came to pay her a visit. I happened to be there at the time, and when I heard Dr Benn's voice in the corridor I slid down into the light-brown leather chair facing my grandmother's hospital bed. Dr Benn had been persistent in reminding me how urgent and imperative it was for me to begin treatment. As I attempted to hide myself, my grandmother was laughing at me from her hospital bed because she couldn't believe that I was eating her diabetic cake – I'd seemed to have forgotten exactly who was the patient.

As she walked into my grandmother's room, Dr Benn noticed me sitting there and her eyes filled with tears.

"You break my heart," she said.

I called her the next day.

———•———

There was something so liberating about me picking up the phone to schedule an appointment with Dr Benn. Perhaps it was because I was finally taking a stand, and changing the negative experience of the diagnosis into the positive one of allowing myself to be saved.

"I'm proud of you," she said.

I had already decided that I was going to opt for a bilateral mastectomy for a couple of reasons: to prevent the cancer returning and spreading to my right breast (as it had with my Aunt Violet), and because I did not want to have to two breasts that were physically different from each other.

Interestingly, the thought that I would be losing my breasts didn't tear me apart as much as the thought of never being able to breastfeed again. I had honestly enjoyed breastfeeding Zenani and Zwelami, even if there was some excitement at stopping as they'd each reached their third year. But for me it was the ultimate expression of my own maternity. I'd loved how both my babies had latched so easily from birth. Thinking about it, I can almost imagine the feeling of full breasts, and how my abundant breast milk would soak up my breast pads. I loved watching both my babies drink, and how they would pull on my nipples with their tiny mouths to the point that they could barely breathe from being so full of my milk.

Sitting in consultation with Dr Benn to discuss the surgery, I mentioned to her that I was worried about waking up to a flat chest after my bilateral mastectomy. It was then that she explained that I could choose an option whereby I wouldn't have to.

Excitement slowly crept into the idea that I could have new breasts. I imagined how I would go under the knife, have my breasts removed and then awake to two perfect C-cups with nipples, like the perfect post-surgery breasts of Dr Rey's clients I'd seen on *Dr. 90210*. But I was still pained, because even though I had always wanted bigger breasts – or perkier ones, after giving birth to three children – I would never have wanted that at the expense of losing their functionality completely.

I still feel like there is something I should have done in memory of my breasts. They'd been with me from the age of eleven to the age of thirty-two, and I wish I could have bid them farewell somehow, and thanked them for allowing me to bond with Zenani and Zwelami in ways I will never be able to with any other child in the years to come. I felt I needed just a little bit more time with them, but there was no longer any sense in postponing the inevitable.

On Monday morning, 2 July 2012, I was once again admitted to the Milpark Hospital – this time for a frozen section bilateral mastectomy with immediate reconstruction. I was dressed all in black from head to toe. I had the privilege of being surrounded by my family by the time I had completed all the paperwork and before my surgery, and I remember only having to look at their faces to be reminded of what was to come. They all sat crowded in their individual chairs facing me in my hospital bed, confined to this small private room in support of my decision to finally get the help I needed.

After the nurse gave me my medical gown and disposable underwear, I went into the bathroom to change. In private, I wanted to capture what would be my last moments with my breasts – the miraculous organs that had fed Zenani and Zwelami for a solid two years each. With my BlackBerry phone I took pictures of my naked breasts from every single angle that I could. It was important not only to say goodbye to them, but I also wanted to remember everything about them and not have to rely on Thierry, who would be the last man to see my natural breasts. When I felt comfortable enough with the number of images I'd taken, I stood in front of the bathroom mirror, moving my body so that I could view them from all angles. And then I stared at them for the last time before saying goodbye, knowing that the next time I walked into that bathroom I would no longer have my breasts.

It wasn't until the nurses walked into my room for the millionth time to take me into theatre that it finally sunk in, and my tears began to stream down my cheeks in full view of my family and the hospital staff.

This moment marked the next phase of my life.

The thought was painful and there wasn't any amount of preparation that would make it any less frightening or real. There was no turning back.

In the holding area my mother and father gave me a kiss goodbye, and I parted ways with Thierry and my family as I was wheeled into theatre. After the anaesthesiologist's brief, I found myself slowly drifting away as the medication took effect and it was only then, as the hospital staff prepared me for my bilateral mastectomy, that I stopped crying.

———•———

Just moments after I regained consciousness I felt tremendous pain and discomfort. It felt as if a ton of bricks had been placed on my chest – it was so tight.

I dozed off again en route back to the hospital room. When next I opened my eyes there was my family and Thierry in the room with me. For my pain I was given morphine in the form of a drip that I could control myself – the drug was released at just the press of a black button on a dark-grey control which I held in my left hand.

The first feelings I experienced in my chest area were tightness and soreness. I remember that the first time I took a peek at my chest I noticed that I wasn't as flat chested as I had anticipated, and I couldn't wait to have Thierry take pictures so I could see myself properly. But nothing made me happier than pressing the black button of my morphine pump. There was never a moment that I wasn't in pain. It became less unbearable towards the end, but as long as I had access to that pump I would be clicking it like someone clicking a BIC pen when they're trying to think. I even joked about how great it felt to be taking legal drugs, and I wondered whether that would constitute a relapse since by then I had been clean and sober for well over a year.

Dressed in a white surgical bra with tubes protruding from the incisions of my new man-made breasts, I stayed in hospital for three days and two nights, all of which Thierry spent with me. Thierry laughed at the sight of my blue and very big disposal underwear, and he teased me about it until I could laugh it off myself – I really looked hideous. With the support of my close family and friends, though, the time went by almost too quickly. Before I knew it I was back home, attached to the same dreaded drainage system –

just, this time, with plastic tubes coming out of both of my breasts.

At home I had to bathe yet again in a bath filled with shallow water and, as advised by the doctor and nurses who had looked after me, I steered clear of my healing wounds. Thierry would assist me with getting out of the bath as I couldn't do it myself without feeling the most excruciating pain in my very weak breast muscles.

In fact, Thierry handled everything from Zwelami to running the house and everything in between.

I found the sight of the fluid being drained by the surgical drain repulsive, so I became quite obsessed with ensuring that all the fluids flowed directly into the pouch and didn't stay trapped anywhere in the plastic tubes. But my distress was not only physical – emotionally I was feeling very sensitive and vulnerable, and I constantly needed Thierry's affection to make me feel loved. Thierry was so afraid of causing me pain that he refrained from touching me too much, and despite his care I was left with the feeling that he found me repulsive. My own helplessness was causing me a lot of stress and frustration.

Five days after the mastectomy I was back at the hospital, and for a change Zwelami came along with Thierry. It was time to remove the drainage system and its attached tubes, and I couldn't wait to gain more mobility – the appointment couldn't come soon enough. Although I still wouldn't be able to drive, lift heavy objects or do any of my usual work around the house, at least I would no longer have an appendage – or my "handbag", as the nurses jokingly called it. But I still cried a river of tears as they removed the tubes

– the sharp, unbearable pain had my son holding my hand while he stood next to my hospital bed. I could literally feel each tube as it was yanked from what felt like the core of my breasts, all the way backwards to the incision.

Dr Slabbert was the plastic surgeon for the breast reconstruction, and as soon as I saw him that day I pounced on him, asking when we could commence filling my breast expanders because I so desperately wanted to start looking and feeling normal. He advised that it would be better for us to wait the three or four weeks until I had completely healed before he could consider adding the saline solution to them.

Back at home, I still had to wear the elasticated white medical bra, which I hated because it always showed through the tops I wore, and I couldn't exactly wear a scarf when it was so hot outside. Of course I couldn't work out at the gym anymore and so I wasn't boxing with my trainer. Although my hard abs were proof of the work I had already put in, I was starting to feel restless and demotivated at the same time.

At an appointment with Dr Benn a few days later, she chatted to me about a possible cup size while she changed my dressing. I was surprised when she said I could actually go as big as a C-plus cup if I fancied, and I loved the idea – I had always wanted something bigger than my 34B cup.

But there were less enticing matters to discuss at that appointment too. Because it was then that I had to finally confirm that I would receive chemotherapy. If so, I would be referred to Dr Georgia Demetriou for genetic testing of my breast tissue, and to figure out the way ahead for my breast cancer treatment.

This was it. I had finally made the decision, and I wasn't going to look back. After the bilateral mastectomy, the worst part about my experience of cancer was officially over.

Or so I thought.

Chapter 24

EXACTLY TWENTY-TWO DAYS after my mastectomy, I noticed how I was able to control movement of both of my breasts. As I moved them up and down, they would change shape, although the muscles in the right breast were much stronger than in the left. I remember standing in front of the mirror repeating the movements over and over again till exhaustion. Never with my natural breasts had I been able to flex them as visibly as I now could with my tissue expanders. I couldn't wait to share this milestone with Thierry.

The scars from my mastectomy were visible from end to end of each breast – on each there was a dark line, with no nipples in sight.

"Does that mean you're a paraplegic now?" Thierry

would tease me, and we'd laugh hysterically at the idea that I actually had no real breasts or nipples. He would talk about how they used to look and how he thought they were just perfect the way they were, before kissing the places where my nipples should have been. If I was feeling strange and different it was never because of Thierry, who made me feel sexy even when I was at my lowest.

But despite the jokes we managed to make at what I considered to be my added flaws, I was still struggling. It was hard not to focus more on what had been taken away from my body, rather than the second chance I have been given.

———

Tuesday, 24 July would officially introduce me to Dr Demetriou, a female oncologist based at the Donald Gordon Medical Centre in Parktown. My grandmother, my Aunt Zenani, my mother and Thierry were all there to support me.

Dr Demetriou calculated that I had a seventy-four per cent chance of the cancer returning if I didn't opt for chemotherapy. She went into detail about two particular chemotherapy treatments that were available – one more aggressive than the other. Of course it was the milder one that was more to my liking ... and of course the recommendation for me was that I follow the harsher of the two treatments, the medical term of which is the official though not very descriptive "4AC to 12 doses of Weekly Paclitaxel". Dr Demetriou explained about my hair falling out, among other ghastly symptoms and side effects I could hypothetically experience.

Great, I thought, this cancer is not going to cut me any slack.

It turns out that the hair loss was going to be the least of my problems, and my concern at that point was not even the recommendation that I do the harsher of the two chemotherapies.

It was the devastating shock of hearing that the chemotherapy could destroy my ovaries, making it impossible for me to conceive again.

Adriamycin, aka the "Red Devil", is used to treat many kinds of cancer, including breast, lung, ovarian and bladder cancer. According to Dr Demetriou, despite its toxic effects on the heart muscles (which could even lead to heart failure) this particular type of chemotherapy was more suitable for me. Despite its harsh side effects – changes to the finger- and toenails, discoloured urine, hair loss, short-term memory loss, nausea, loss of appetite, stomach pains, insomnia, sweats, mouth sores, and more – this was how I was going to beat my cancer.

But all that paled in significance as I tried to grasp the notion that I really may not be able to conceive or breastfeed ever again. It just seemed so unfair. To make matters worse, the chemotherapy would force me into early menopause, weaken my heart and cause a very low immune system. And the side effects were not necessarily reversible – that was made very clear to me from the beginning.

Was this going to be my life?

Just like Dr Benn, Dr Demetriou attempted to reassure me. There were alternative measures available for me to have more children, she said, but I felt like I'd already lived a lifetime of pain – and now this.

Why was I living such a horrific nightmare?

I didn't care for sympathy. I just wanted to know why.

"Motherhood is my thing," I told Dr Demetriou – the same words I had spoken earlier to Dr Benn.

The situation was fast becoming surreal. I was becoming conflicted by the choice I had made to get the best treatment available to me, because it now felt as though I was getting the raw end of the deal. It was a catch-22: the more "right" choices I was making to save myself, the worse the consequences were becoming.

Cut off one breast ... and it will come back in the other.

Take aggressive chemotherapy to decrease the chances of the cancer returning ... and increase the likelihood of infertility. And after all that, the cancer might just come back anyway.

I walked out of those rooms absolutely broken.

———

I desperately needed something to go right, and this was the beginning of my increased obsession with my breasts.

It had been six weeks since I had last seen Dr Slabbert, and I was growing impatient at the sight of my small, ready-to-be-filled breasts. I desperately wanted more volume so that I could at least begin filling out my bras and tops.

After making the mistake of jotting his number down incorrectly, I eventually managed to get hold of his office, only to be told that he was on leave and I would have to wait another week or two. I had no option but to be patient until, finally, in late August, Dr Slabbert walked into his consulting room to find Thierry, my grandmother, my Aunt Zenani and Aunt Ntutuzelo, who was looking after my grandmother at the time, sitting waiting with me for my much-anticipated breast fill.

For my first expander fill I asked if we could film the procedure on my BlackBerry. Dr Slabbert began by extracting with an oversized syringe 50cc (cubic centimetres) of saline solution from a saline bag. He then inserted the syringe into the two buttons underneath each breast and slowly began to fill them. Almost immediately there was a change in the contour of my breasts.

But it would take quite a few more fills before I was happy with the size. When I got home that day and reached for my old bra, I realised sadly that my new breasts didn't even begin to fill it.

In early September, after my second breast-fill consultation, which was thirteen days after the first, there was still no huge difference in the size of my breasts – rather, it seemed as if the solution was spreading width ways, rather than outwards as I wanted. By this stage, I was beyond obsessed with breasts – any breasts. I would stare at women's breasts deciding whether they'd be the right fit for me, or what I would change about them if I could. I knew we would get to the final stage of my breast reconstruction gradually – but I wanted it all to happen immediately – blame that on the addict in me, the need for instant gratification.

I was just so eager to have them look the way I wanted them to.

Chapter 25

PERHAPS IT WAS MY OBSESSION with breasts that kept me from dealing with what was even more dear to me.

Dr Benn had recommended that I consult with various fertility clinics so that I could discuss the possibilities of "saving" my eggs before my ovaries were potentially damaged during chemo. Although I was fully aware of the urgency to make contact, it was weeks before I eventually made the call to the Vitalab Centre for Assisted Conception. On 13 September, after I'd filled in yet more forms and documents, my grandmother, Aunt Zenani, Thierry and I walked into their Rivonia rooms and met with Dr Jacobson to discuss the possibility of having more babies when the chemotherapy treatments were done.

I was highly anxious as I sat in the doctor's office, with no inkling of what to expect. Dr Jacobson, a specialist in reproductive medicine and fertility issues, had been involved in the practice of infertility since 1978 and was one of the original founding members of Vitalab. But I was not there for an infertility problem – I was there to conserve what I already had.

Understandably, Dr Jacobson assumed that Thierry and I would want our consultation with him to be private. I felt so uncomfortable when he asked my aunt and grandmother to excuse us, which they did. At my request, though, they returned only minutes later: they had been with me at every other consultation and I explained to Dr Jacobson that I felt it necessary for them to be there. With all of us together, he gave a brief introduction of what options were available to me.

Although Thierry and I had been through so much, the focus had always been on getting me well – although it was an unspoken dream, we had never actually discussed the idea of a having a baby together.

I was taken into another room, where a vaginal scan was performed. Once he'd got a look at my ovaries via the scan, Dr Jacobson mentioned that he suspected I'd had no problems falling pregnant in the past. I burst out laughing and felt immediately comforted. As I'd lain there doubting whether I would ever be fertile again, that was exactly what I needed to hear.

Back in his consulting room, he prepared to send me to the fertility nurse coordinator for contraceptives and to Lancet Laboratories for blood tests. By the time I left for home, I had been given several options that I needed to consider. Would I be prepared to have my ovaries (or a piece of them) surgically removed and then returned to my body after chemotherapy? Would I have just my eggs frozen, or would I have them fertilised first and then frozen?

There were options at least, and the issue of conserving my fertility was not as hopeless as I had envisaged it to be.

Four days after my consultation at the fertility clinic I had my third breast expander fill, on 17 September. I went along with my grandmother, my Aunt Ntutuzelo and Thierry. I specifically asked Thierry to refrain from making any comments as I convinced Dr Slabbert to increase the fill to 60cc as opposed to the planned 50cc, and I strongly feel that if it weren't for Thierry, I would have had even more injected into my expanders. He's completely against me getting a size larger than my 34B which he prefers.

Although I'd always felt that my upper body was not in proportion with my lower body, Dr Slabbert didn't think my breasts would suit my frame if I went too big. He didn't want me to leave with dodgy-looking breasts, or with breasts that were rock hard after overfilling, as opposed to being as soft and natural-looking as they now were. He spoke about visual aesthetics and tactile aesthetics – and that the feel and weight of the breast was as important as its size. By the time he had filled my second breast it was quite clear that this would be my last fill. This upset me.

When he was finished, my grandmother commented on how in proportion they were, to which I asked cheekily whether she had seen my buttocks – they didn't match. When Dr Slabbert heard that, he immediately told me that I should not compensate for one thing with another – which is true, as that is probably exactly what I had been doing in my quest for a perfect rack.

With the breast reconstruction almost complete, it was time for me to begin looking at the fertility issue in earnest.

Back at the Vitalab clinic in early October for my second consultation with Dr Jacobson, I was told that my blood tests had indicated that I had an underactive thyroid – my thyroid gland was not producing enough of certain important hormones, upsetting the normal balance. In my case, a slow thyroid meant that it would be more difficult to fall pregnant because I was not ovulating normally, and I would have to take a daily tablet to replace the thyroxin hormone.

I felt I was in safe hands, and so began an intense process which I was beginning to see as my own insurance – protecting not just my chances of having a baby, but of possibly having Thierry's baby.

A week later, Dr Jacobson discussed the cost breakdown of my fertility treatment before referring us to Sister Anne Hacking, the programme and fertility nurse coordinator at Vitalab.

At this stage, it started to feel as if Thierry and I were practically living at the clinic. We were going so often that it would have been way too exhausting for my Aunt Zenani and grandmother to accompany us every time, so from then on we started going together as a couple.

The following day, Dr Jacobson performed yet another vaginal scan and I was given my first Menopur injection by Sister Anne – the first of eight that I would end up having. It is Menopur that contains the hormones that stimulate healthy ovaries to make eggs and is known to be administered to women who need medical assistance for falling pregnant – over the coming weeks, if Menopur was not given to me subcutaneously at Vitalab, then it was injected by Thierry wherever we were.

I had to start antibiotics and antifungals – particularly Ciprofloxacin, which I took twice daily, and Fluconazole. As dehydration affects fertility, I had to increase my fluid intake from my usual two litres of water a day to two-and-a-half or three litres.

Thierry and I soon had an introductory session with Bernice List, the resident counsellor at the facility, which served as an icebreaker of sorts, because we got to know Bernice quite well. In her office, Sister Anne administered my second dose of Menopur by injecting it into my stomach. She showed Thierry how to do it, as he would soon begin administering the Menopur from the five-day kit we were given.

Three days later, Thierry and I had our second counselling session with Bernice. Although I'd been avoiding thinking about it, this would be our last session before chemotherapy began. A cancer survivor herself, Bernice was so helpful in going through the practical aspects of chemotherapy, as well as our relationship dynamics. But no amount of talk could hide my feelings of fear about the chemotherapy procedure itself, which loomed, scary and unknowable, in the future. There was obviously a whole lot to be concerned about, and there were many times that Thierry and I went from being absolutely sure about the way forward, to sitting alone in our own little corners questioning the roles we'd need to play in this movie we'd been cast in.

In the meantime, there was so much to do, and so many details to take care of, that we diligently followed our instructions in almost a haze. There is something strange about being kept busy in this way, and sometimes I forgot exactly why I was doing all his – the bigger picture seemed to fade into the background as we concerned ourselves with clinic visits, daily tablets and numberless injections.

The following day was a Tuesday, and Thierry and I returned to Vitalab, where another vaginal scan was performed. We were told that, based on that scan, we could possibly begin the egg retrieval process the following week. I was then sent to Lancet for yet another blood test.

We were finding ourselves at the clinic a number of times a week, and sometimes even more than once a day. Sitting in the open-plan waiting room we saw the same couples over and over again, faces that were becoming so familiar. Although we all knew there was heartbreak in our various stories, I soon learnt that not all problems are created equal, and that we all have our crosses to bear.

As we were awaiting our turn with the doctor, one woman asked me whether Thierry and I were also trying for a baby. I don't recall the exact conversation, but I do remember how quickly I felt I needed to explain my story to her: that I was not at Vitalab because I had infertility issues, but because I might not be able to conceive once I had finished chemotherapy. I suppose so much had gone wrong in my life that I didn't want to take on the mantle of infertility as well, when it was the one thing I had never had trouble with. For whatever reason, it was important for me to let her know that, but once I'd told her she quickly reclined into her seat and looked completely disinterested in whatever else I had to say.

On the Wednesday I was given an additional shot of Menopur and also Cetrotide. This medication, which Thierry would have to administer to me in conjunction with

Menopur, is usually given on stimulation day five or seven – it assists in controlling the body's hormonal response, which then affects the development of eggs so that they reach the level of development required for fertilisation.

By the Thursday my ovaries had produced over fourteen eggs each. Our consultation with Sister Anne entailed two more injections for me. An egg retrieval kit had already been ordered, and would be used on the day of the retrieval.

After all that we'd been through, Thierry and I felt that we really needed a break, and so we decided to take a weekend off to go to our family lodge at Shambala, near Vaalwater, with some of my family. We were given a cooler box with the medication I would need for our trip.

But there was no real way of "getting away", and we had to leave for Johannesburg at five in the morning that Saturday to make it for an eight o'clock appointment at Vitalab, to return to Shambala immediately afterwards. By then, a vaginal scan revealed that I was producing over eighteen eggs in one ovary and over sixteen in the other. Sister Anne then gave Thierry and me a demonstration on how to administer a new medication called Lucrin, which ripens the eggs and which, like the Menopur, is also given via an injection into the fatty tissue under the skin of my stomach.

As everything was going according to plan, it was confirmed that the egg retrieval would be that Tuesday. There were more documents to be signed and bills to be paid. I was sent to Lancet for another blood test.

By the Monday, we were back at home, and this time when we went to the clinic, I did not require a vaginal scan for a change, although I still had to make my way to Lancet for another blood test. Sister Anne administered my last shot of forty units of Lucrin, which was in addition to the forty units Thierry had administered the night before. The next day was the official day of the surgery, and at this point I looked like I was carrying a three-month pregnancy. I was feeling extremely uncomfortable and after all the medication and injections my uterus was bordering on painful.

In anticipation of the egg retrieval procedure, I was given a sheet of paper with the instruction not to eat any solid food for six hours before the procedure, and no liquids for four hours before the procedure.

Chapter 26

ON THE MORNING OF MY EGG retrieval, Thierry and I arrived at Vitalab at seven. There were a few leather armchairs on my left – where, I assumed, many women had sat waiting to leave after surgery. To my right were three beds, each with a chair beside it and a beige zinc cabinet for patients to place their belongings while in theatre.

It was strange to be in yet another ward and to wear yet another hospital gown. I had to change into it twice, because for some reason I couldn't figure out how I was supposed to put it on, despite the countless times the nurses told me. My body was there, but my mind was clearly elsewhere. In the end, I wore one covering my front, tied at the back, and one covering my back, tied at the front. The gowns are not exactly glamorous, but at least I was well and truly covered!

Preparations for my surgery went quickly and, after filling out some basic questions on a form, I was soon wheeled into theatre, for the oocyte (egg cell) removal. A needle is attached to an internal ultrasound probe, which is used to see the ovaries and find the ovarian follicle after being inserted into the vagina. The needle punctures each follicle and sucks out the follicle's liquid, after which an embryologist will evaluate the fluid in order to find the egg.

I would be under sedation the whole time, and I do not remember anything from the time the assisting nurse said, "Happy sleeping ..."

The surgery took just a quarter of an hour, and then I was wheeled back to the ward on my hospital bed. But it felt like hours for me to come round. When I finally awoke fully, there was Thierry, sitting in the same chair I'd left him in when I'd been wheeled out.

It was the greatest feeling to find a plaster on my left palm with a smiley face and the words "28 eggs – well done!" written in a black marker. I recalled some nurses telling me that on average they retrieve seven to eleven eggs from each patient. While I was coming round, Sister Anne had mentioned to Thierry that I had quite a lot of eggs, and one of the nurses had said that I'd literally broken a record! That explained why they were clapping as they came into the ward: they had retrieved twenty-eight eggs of the thirty-plus I had officially produced.

That was something to proud of and it made me so happy. It reminded me of how the doctor had jokingly told me I should be called Mother Hen due to how fertile I was.

I was told I needed to eat half an hour after the procedure, and that I could only be discharged once I'd passed urine – which took quite a while, despite the copious amounts of water I was drinking. If ever I experienced any problems such as pain in the chest, stomach or neck, I would have to contact my doctor immediately.

Just as I was leaving I was hit with nausea that made me want to throw up right there in the car park – but strangely enough, by the time I arrived home I managed to stomach a Big Mac, large fries and an orange juice for my first post-surgery meal.

By then, I was not just experiencing discomfort. The pain meds administered to me at Vitalab had worn off, and I was in a considerable amount of pain. I took some painkillers, but that night was excruciating.

The next day I could expect a call from Vitalab to inform me about the status of my eggs.

Although Sister Anne and Dr Jacobson had advised that I would only begin with chemotherapy forty-eight hours after my oocyte removal, the wait to begin my treatment was proving more unbearable with each passing day.

My feeling was that the sooner I got started, the sooner I could be done with it all, and I could not bear to wait another second, minute or hour. I deliberately scheduled my first chemotherapy treatment for the very next day.

October 24, 2012 marked the life-changing day that I would start my first cycle of chemotherapy at the Wits Donald Gordon Medical Centre in Parktown.

PART III

Woman,
You carry life's tribulations and false impressions
On your shoulders, heavy with dissatisfaction
Back arched, your limp leaves a sequence of bad choices
and foolishness.
You are so quick to charge
That which you do not desire in relation to yourself
Continues to stare you in the face.
A reflection of yourself, you choose to conceal
In your injury, you've shifted the blame
And in your melancholy, you drown.
You cry the tears of woman who on the sly
Cry by night and smile the smiles of fresh mothers,
Longing for the status of those whose lives He's touched,
Yet you do not seek and desire His direction?
He has caught your tears ... and He carries your
continuation,
For your life, remains his enduring equation.

What once escorted your misplaced ways and sunken
sentiment

Lives now, a woman in the course of action.
You who now lies beside your spawn
Heart clenched, thankful because you know Him,
From the words that drip off your tongue,
To the lives around you that manufacture and attach each
unit of your nucleus
To the reconstruction of your demeanour.
She is, the coming of herself
She is, where she needs to be
She is, you!
It is at His request, that your life follows His design
For you were chosen, countless times over.

So rise, my sister ... Rise!
For you are a fusion of unbroken blessings,
For you are of the very essence.
Let your energy rise to fill the hearts that hold you up
For you are a diamond,
Shine your significance and radiate the light of your rebirth.
Dance to your own beat for your melody echoes His arrival
Your rhythm, an indication of self-adoration and
indebtedness.
Look at all that is around you, that through Him you give
meaning to.

It is your time to stand up!

~ Zoleka Mandela

Chapter 27

First chemotherapy treatment (fifteen to go)

As ARRANGED WITH DR DEMETRIOU, two nurses meet me and Thierry in the parking lot of the Donald Gordon Medical Centre, and take us to a private room in the oncology ward. Walking in there, I'm feeling worried and scared.

I don't know what to expect.

A blood test to check my blood sugar level is done with a prick to my finger, and my temperature is taken. And then Dr Demetriou arrives to talk me through what is going to happen today, and what symptoms I can expect afterwards.

I am going to have a cocktail of chemotherapy medications administered to me intravenously: 105mg of Adriamycin (also known as the "Red Devil"), which prevents the cancer from generating new DNA; 1050mg of Cyclophosphamide; 20mg of Decadron; and 3mg of Kytril. I'll initially take 125mg of Emend orally (this prevents nausea), and I'll have a 10-8mg injection of Zoladex, which will reduce my body's level of oestrogen, thus triggering menopause and causing the tumours to shrink. She tells me I should expect constipation, mouth ulcers, blackening of the nail bed, darkening of the area where the drip was inserted, watery eyes, a runny nose and darkened spots on the palms and tongue.

Today is Wednesday. By Friday the medication will have worn off and I may begin to feel a dip. I should expect my hair to start falling out in patches in two to three weeks.

It is going to be relentless.

She tells me that my next chemotherapy treatment is scheduled for three weeks' time, and I can expect to have a blood test before each session to determine my white blood cell count and whether my immune system is strong enough to handle that day's chemo. My immune system will be low. My heart will be weak.

I am weak at the thought.

The first four chemotherapy treatments would be given to me every three weeks – these will have the most potent side effects. They'll be followed by twelve sessions, which will take place every week. In total, the course will be for the duration of six months.

I am first given the Zoladex injection and am shocked at the size of the needle. It leaves behind a noticeable hole in the skin on my stomach.

Half an hour later, the other drugs are hooked, one by one, into the IV, and I sit in a relaxed upright position on the remote-controlled bed until the early afternoon, receiving the medication that is going to save my life.

By the time I get home I'm almost feeling normal.

Then, as I am attempting to clean the house, a sudden bout of nausea hits me and turns my world upside down. It doesn't help one bit that I am still in quite a lot of pain from yesterday's oocyte retrieval. Now, I experience a feeling of bloating, stomach cramps, discomfort urinating and the worst nausea I have ever had in my life.

That's when I receive the call from Vitalab: the call to inform me of how many eggs they have managed to freeze. My heart sinks as I hear the number. I expected the number to be far more than the specialist tells me, although she assures me that the result is very good under the circumstances. I suppose I should be more grateful, but I'm genuinely disappointed. After all those injections, I produced over thirty eggs, had twenty-eight extracted, and the number just keeps going down.

I'm getting so cheesed off with these highs and lows – one moment I am basking in some success, only to have any happiness shattered.

At Uncle Alf Kumalo's memorial service the day after my chemo I am almost immobilised by the pain. I feel I have to be there, though, and there is nothing or no one that could have stopped me from going. Afterwards, I can't even walk upright back to the car, or sit upright once I've got in. Just touching my stomach causes such pain, and it doesn't matter what position I'm in, or how much I reposition myself, it feels like the pain is getting more intense by the moment.

This is what drinking poison must feel like.

The car ride back home is unbelievable. Each time the driver stops, or makes a turn, or – even worse – goes over a speed bump, the pain gets worse. I am in the back seat, one arm on the arm rest and one clutching my lower body as I squirm in pain. Chemotherapy is no joke, I realise. I am crying tears of pain, and this is only from the first treatment.

How am I going to last fifteen more? Is it even possible?

I am almost certain this pain is from constipation. When my Aunt Zenani tells me to pass by her place to collect some natural laxatives, I do – and immediately take more than what is recommended.

It does not help at all.

By the fifth day I am at least able to resume my duties as the home's chef, although my nausea is triggered by every single thing I do, including preparing meals. Sometimes I can't even stomach a glass of water, let alone any other liquids. Food aversions. The food I love so much has become a mission to eat and I hate every bite. I lose two kilograms in a week.

I've also had to remove my artificial lashes, since I expect them to fall off soon anyway, and I've had the acrylic on my nails soaked off. I am officially going "all natural".

I can't handle being fully clothed, so I've opted for wearing a sarong around my waist, which I pull up when Zwelami is around.

I'm feeling like I have pregnancy symptoms on steroids, and everything is accompanied with jutting pain. Sometimes I find myself in a foetal position praying for it all to be over because I don't think I can last another day feeling this way.

It's now seven days after my first chemotherapy treatment.

I'm no longer experiencing the excruciating stomach cramps, constipation, headaches, nausea or bloating. Instead, I'm now suffering from heartburn and indigestion. Luckily, these are easily cured with bicarbonate of soda – a trick I discover on the Internet. I mix just less than a teaspoonful in a little cup of water, and I burp almost as soon as I've drunk it – giving instant relief.

When I'm not dealing with that, I'm treating my mouth ulcer, which has reappeared twice in the same place. The saline solution my oncologist recommended has worked wonders, and I've been advised to always keep my mouth clean and to remember to gargle with the saline solution after every meal to stop it from reoccurring. I now keep a two-litre Valpré bottle filled with the solution in the bathroom next to the sink.

As expected, I've also started noticing the darkening of the vein which was used for my chemo, as well as the skin of my lips.

On the eleventh day I am able to start driving, and I take advantage of that by running errands and working out – albeit moderately.

I know it's a strange thing to notice, but it's around now that I realise I'm not producing any earwax, which scares the living daylights out of me because anyone who knows me knows my fear of insects.

Paranoia.

If I'm not producing earwax, then insects will find their way into my ears, I'm sure.

And then I start losing my hair.

On Tuesday, 6 November 2012 – the very same day that the man who drove my daughter the night she was killed is acquitted of all charges – I walk into my local hair salon. The visit would, under normal circumstances, be long overdue, but it's more necessary now than ever: it's just less than two weeks after my first chemotherapy treatment.

The hairdresser removes my weave and takes out the wool from the cornrows on my head. It is only as he starts combing out the plaits that I notice that the hair on my scalp is literally dropping out in patches: my hair is being lifted into the air by the comb only to land up on the floor. Each time it does, I glance around to see if anyone else in the salon is watching.

At some point, I have to ask the hairdresser to stop. Although I didn't know what to expect when I left home, I packed my lace wig to wear after my weave had been removed, and it's now come in handy.

When I get up from the chair on my way to go and pay, I see all my hair on the floor. And then I don't look back again, in case my eyes accidentally meet everyone else's shocked faces.

It's not until I get home and remove my lace wig that I now give my natural hair a thorough inspection. I try to run my fingers through my hair, only to land up with chunks of hair coming away between my fingers.

I burst into tears.

Crying my eyes out, I call Thierry to tell him how my hair is coming out in patches.

Thierry later arrives with Zwelami, who he has picked up from school as he often does if I am unable to. I hear them walking up the stairs, and I am standing in my bathroom looking at what is left of my hair when they walk in.

Thierry takes one look at me and bursts into uncontrollable laughter.

This has been one of the worst days of my life. I have just heard that the driver in the accident that killed my daughter is a free man. Now here I am in the bathroom in the worst state I have ever been in. In walks Thierry and he bursts in to laughter when he sees my hair. "Oh shit! It does look fucked up!"

The next thing I know, Zwelami is behind me with a comb in one hand, trying to give me a Mohawk.

There was something about this moment, because within seconds I am in stitches of laughter as I surrender to the absurdity of the whole situation. As Thierry and Zwelami take turns trying to style my hair into a Mohawk, I begin relating my experience at the hair salon. I don't know how many times I have to tell Thierry that there is no way I'm going to let him use his clippers on me – he's waiting for the go-ahead like a kid in a candy store. He's been dying to give me a Mohawk with his clippers and can never keep a straight face about it.

Today there is no more crying about the loss of my hair, although in the next few weeks I will develop a bit of a "thing" about my hair. I'm putting what is left of it in plaits, and every morning I comb them out before plaiting them again. I keep the hair that falls out in a hairnet – I think I am somehow expecting it to reattach itself to my scalp after God knows what.

When I tell my Aunt Zenani about this, she insists that I give her the hairnet and she burns it.

———◆———

Eighteen days after my first chemotherapy treatment I make my way to my Aunt Zenani's home so that my cousin-in-law can shave my head.

We sit down together and I have my head shaved in full view of some members of my family. They're there to support me, along with my dear friend Thatohatsi, who I've been friends with since primary school. She has her head shaved in my honour at the same time – as a new friend of mine, Zintle, has done, although Zintle is not at the house today. I ask Zwelami to record my home-made Shavathon on my phone while everyone else watches to see what I'll look like, and how I'll react once I see myself in the mirror.

"You look just like Daddy Oupa!" my cousins and my Aunt Zenani say.

But when I eventually see my bald head, I'm in tears once again and for the rest of the day until I arrive home a few hours later.

I've had an argument with Thierry, which is why he wasn't there with me at my Aunt Zenani's place with the rest of the family. Neither is he at my place once Zwelami and I arrive home. But, as I've discovered, painful moments like this are mixed with some hilarious ones that catch me totally off guard. Like when I look back after using the toilet, only to find that most of my pubic hair has fallen into it. Instant Hollywood wax, thanks to chemotherapy!

There is nothing to do but laugh at the peculiarity of it all – and, most of the time, Thierry laughs just as hard with me.

———◆———

Exactly nineteen days after my first chemotherapy treatment I take a few pictures of my bald head and post them on BlackBerry Messenger and Facebook. I can't begin to explain how immensely proud I am the moment people's messages started pouring in. Their show of encouragement and support on this particular day is not the first I will encounter, nor is it the last.

I feel so liberated and empowered: Cancer has taken my hair, but how little it knows me if it thinks I will be broken by that.

Chapter 28

Second chemotherapy treatment (fourteen to go)

THIERRY AND I DROP ZWELAMI off at school and head back to the Donald Gordon Medical Centre for my second chemotherapy treatment. We arrive almost an hour before the appointment, so we sit in the car waiting, where I record a video on my iPad about how I'm feeling – something I have started doing regularly.

Then we decide to go for breakfast at the centre's downstairs café. I opt for the biggest slice of red-velvet cake, which I finish to the last crumb, and a cup of hot chocolate before we head in. Kim, the centre's public relations officer, meets us in the reception area – as she will almost every time from now on – to take us to a private room upstairs. My grandmother, my mother and Sis' Zodwa, my grandmother's personal assistant, arrive together, and my Aunt Zenani joins us upstairs a few minutes later. My brother Zondwa arrives shortly after her.

A nurse from Lancet Laboratories arrives, and my blood is taken and blood sugar checked, followed by my blood pressure and temperature. A bit later, Dr Demetriou walks in with the results of my blood tests, which indicate that we can begin with the second treatment.

As usual, the drugs are lined up on a trolley outside my hospital room in the order in which they must be administered. The treatment goes as can be expected – although the headache I get during the treatment makes me uncomfortable.

—◆—

I should have known it was too good to be true.

The day after the second chemotherapy treatment, I have already reverted to doing my chores around the house when I am hit with a bout of nausea, only slightly more bearable than the last time.

On the third day, I am in bed feeling sick to my stomach as the other side effects rear their ugly heads. I am lying flat on my back in a sarong with the fan aimed directly at me. My own scent is enough to make me throw up and there is no telling everything that triggers my nausea.

At the second treatment Dr Demetriou asked me whether I had been experiencing any hot flushes, and her description of them was exactly what I am feeling right now. There is a sudden hotness that starts at the top of my head and then warms up my face and then my whole body, causing me to sweat. In the next few days I start to experience night sweats so bad that in the middle of the night I have to turn over my pillow because it is drenched.

And still there is the heartburn, nausea and headaches that make being in a car challenging, although Gaviscon and a few painkillers and some home remedies do well to alleviate the discomfort.

My veins hurt when I apply body lotion after a shower, or if Thierry accidently touches my arm. Although my head has already been shaved, my hair somehow hasn't fallen out completely, and I constantly find traces of it on my pillow in the mornings, and on my face or neck, especially when I run my hands over my scalp.

At Zwelami's school carol service I am so sick. Sitting outside in the heat of mid-summer, I am literally nauseated by every smell. A week after that, I start noticing the dark bruising on the nailbeds of both my thumbs, and my freckles seem to be migrating all over my face, which is left looking patchy.

I forgot to buy the sunscreen that my oncologist so strongly recommended, and so the skin on my face has been slightly burnt by the sun. My hands and feet are becoming darker than the rest of my body – partly because of the chemo, but more so because of the lack of sunscreen.

And did I mention the increased forgetfulness?

Thatohatsi has organised a girl's evening at her home. I spend most of the night either sitting on my hands, or hiding them between my crossed legs. My skin looks so dark – especially tonight.

I am wearing heels, and I can't stop staring at the skin of my feet, which is darker than ever. Somehow, painting my fingernails has made my hands appear even darker, and it looks like my hands and feet belong to a completely different person.

I can't wait to go into hiding in my own home.

I haven't worn my tongue ring in ages. When I check my tongue, I am shocked to discover that it looks bruised and dirty, or stained as if I've been drinking red wine. These symptoms are all expected, but nothing prepares you for the shock of seeing your body change so drastically, so quickly.

I also develop a urinary tract infection, which is common, and which requires a prescription for antibiotics from my doctor. It clears within several days, but until then urinating is unbearable. After this, I will constantly get urinary tract infections – it is part of the chemotherapy package.

Just days before my next scheduled chemotherapy treatment I develop a slight cough and start feeling constantly and overly exhausted.

Chapter 29

Third chemotherapy treatment (thirteen to go)

MY THIRD CHEMOTHERAPY TREATMENT is postponed from 5
to 11 December because my white blood cell count is low.
My immune system has taken a beating. I feel so bad about
having my grandmother, my Aunt Zenani, Thierry and Sis'
Zodwa there for me, only to be sent home without treatment.

Before I leave, I am given a Neulastim injection on the
right side of my stomach. It will boost my white blood cell
count and reduce the risk of infection, but Dr Demetriou
warns that it will cause bone pain. To minimise my exposure
to germs, I also have to bring home a box of latex gloves
to wear, a box of medical masks for me to wear when I'm
around other people, and a 500ml bottle of alcohol hand

rub, with instructions to use it frequently. Dr Demetriou tells me to avoid sick people, public places and flowers.

I will also need to follow a low-bacteria diet for the next week, before we resume with the chemotherapy. A nurse gives me a green-coloured low-bacteria food guide: in it are guidelines about what types of food I should eat to boost my weakened immune system, along with the way foods should be prepared and served. Uncooked foods are most likely to contain bacteria and fungi, which then pose a higher risk to an "immune-suppressed patient" – that is now me. I am allowed absolutely *no* raw or undercooked animal foods; no uncooked fish, smoked salmon, sushi or shellfish; no moldy cheese; no raw vegetables, salads or fruits; no nuts, including peanut butter; no seeds; no chocolate containing nuts and seeds; no breads; no cereal; no stale foods and no foods past their use-by date. Whatever meals and drinks I do have – *What is there left to eat?* I wonder – has to be properly wrapped or covered.

It doesn't help that Thierry has developed a cold and has to be extra cautious around me. Later, in my bedroom, to keep me company while keeping a distance, he spends the evening sitting on my brown leather chair wearing one of the medical masks I've been given.

Towards the end of the evening I am beginning to feel the side effects of the Neulastim: a severe headache and back pain start developing and soon I am consumed by extreme pain. I can't bear to have Thierry sleep in the guest room, so he sleeps at my feet, wearing his medical mask all night, as I will for a number of days.

—◆—

The anti-inflammatory Celebrex medication that I was given

to treat the side effects of the Neulastim booster gives me a taste of what it feels like to have chronic arthritis. For the next few days I walk around the house like an old lady with stiff joints. Although the pain comes in spasms – which feel like contractions of my spinal cord and head – it might as well be constant. I need to sleep in a semi-upright position because it is too painful to lean my back against my headboard or lie down completely flat. It feels like someone is tugging at the nerves inside my spinal cord as they would the strings on a puppet; I can do nothing to stop the spasms and I have no control over how long they last. When the pain in my back subsides, my head throbs so much that I feel like I can hear the pain.

I squint my eyes to try and relieve the pressure, but there is no relief.

Not too long after the pain subsides, my urinary tract infection flares up again, along with my mouth ulcer. Thierry calls to my attention a rash that I suddenly develop on the back of my head, caused by all the medication.

I am discovering first-hand what it means to have a weakened immune system. I accidentally bite the inside of my cheek, and although days go by, my wound does not heal – a fact that I am reminded of each time I eat, drink or brush my teeth. My body is no longer able to heal itself. It is extremely uncomfortable and painful, and I turn to painkillers, despite having weaned myself off them after my last surgery for fear of becoming cross-addicted.

I soon discover the painkillers I'm using are not strong enough – and Thierry has to rush to the pharmacy down the road to get me something even stronger.

They only dull the extremity of the pain.

On 11 December, on the way to the medical centre for my rescheduled chemotherapy session, Thierry gives me the longest lecture about how upset he will be with me if the results show that there has been no improvement to my immune system. He feels that I haven't been one hundred per cent cautious in the week leading up to the chemo.

Last week, I wanted to attend the funeral of one of my grandmother's bodyguards, despite being advised by Dr Demetriou to avoid large crowds where I could be in contact with too many people, or people who may be sick, and who could pose a threat to my compromised immune system. In the end I had bargained with Thierry: I visited the bodyguard's home on the morning of the funeral to pay my respects to his family and to extend my apologies for not attending the funeral itself.

Now, my family and I return to the medical centre to have Dr Demetriou disclose good news from my blood tests: my immune system is up, and I can continue my treatment as scheduled. Even better, she feels it's desirable for me to take a break during the festive season – so my December appointment will be the last one of the year. I couldn't have had the year end any better. Although I'm anxious to reach the end of this road, I am sure the break will do me good, and I agree to resume treatment in January 2013.

I am also so relieved to hear that I can revert to a proper diet, and that I don't have to wear the mask twenty-four seven to protect myself. Dr Demetriou mentions that I can expect my hair to start growing back after the fourth chemo treatment and that I should begin loading up on vitamin-B supplements.

As usual, my "matriarchs" – my grandmother and Aunt Zenani – are there to support me, along with Thierry and Sis' Zodwa. They all sit on chairs surrounding my hospital bed and engage in interesting topics of conversation, with Sis' Zodwa never shying from sharing various biblical scriptures with me. Every session starts a different discussion, and a few contagious laughs are shared.

They are my light in all of this.

The day after the chemo, I wake up with the usual nausea – but not so bad that I can't drive myself to the petrol station to buy a few items I need for the house. It's a triumph for anti-nausea medication, and I wonder how cancer patients like my Aunt Violet survived chemotherapy without it. How did people cope with nausea back in the day, when it is so hard to deal with nausea even *with* anti-nausea medication?

Two days later I am on a flight home to Qunu in the Eastern Cape to support my younger brother, Bambatha – or *umkhwetha*, as an initiate is known – who is in the midst of his rite of passage. Although I have been ill from the chemotherapy, I would not have been able to forgive myself for missing this highlight of my brother's life, and I want to be a part of it. During my stay at my grandfather's house, I still experience nausea and night sweats. I feel sick and I am constantly tired, but I know that the next chemotherapy treatment will mark the end of the worst ones.

I cannot help but look forward.

My hair has started growing back. It is extremely thin and is the strangest colour.

Normally I have dark-brown hair, but I don't think that anyone – not even my family – has seen my natural hair. Even

I have only seen it sporadically at hair salons when changing my weave. For a long time I hated my hair because all the weaving, braiding, relaxing and perming over the years has made it weak – so, for anyone else, the sight has been taboo.

I'm comforted by the new growth, though none of what is now returning to my scalp resembles what I've come to see as my natural hair.

Chapter 30

Fourth chemotherapy treatment (twelve to go)
WE ARE ALL BACK TO THE DONALD Gordon Medical Centre on 9 January for my fourth treatment – the first one of 2013.

It is a day over four weeks since the last chemo session, and I've been feeling more normal than I have for a long time. My matriarchs are here again, but Sis' Zodwa has had to attend to other family matters and has not been able to make it. Once again, I'm taken to a private room in one of the wings of the hospital, although it's a different one from last time. The new year also brings with it new medical staff – I haven't until now realised how attached I had become to those who were assigned to me during the last three treatments.

I didn't have a chance to eat breakfast in this morning's rush to get here, but the kitchen staff provide a spread of sandwiches, tea and coffee that we all help ourselves to. One of the male nurses comes in after responding to the nurse's bell and I ask for some more refreshments. He replies, "Two coffees, one tea and one chemo!" and I laugh as he stops just short of saying, "Coming right up!" before heading out of the room. No matter how serious the treatment is, there is always space for a laugh and a hug shared among my family and the nursing staff taking care of me.

A little while later, Dr Demetriou walks into the room and informs us that, as was explained to me previously, this is going to be the last of the four "major" treatments, and that I'll return on 30 January to start a course of weekly sessions every Wednesday for twelve weeks. I ask her why my last treatment resulted in barely any serious side effects, and she tells me she believes it is due to the white blood cell booster she gave me. I am incredibly touched when she then hugs me, and tells me that she's proud of me, and how she's found my attitude towards everything particularly great.

The chemotherapy takes so much longer this time around. During the session, I notice that my hot flushes are more frequent than usual. I still can't believe that I am menopausing at 32. Afterwards, the nausea rears its ugly face right there in my hospital bed – way before I even get home. I am also extremely tired and find myself dozing off every now and then, which I normally only do when I get into the car to go home. I am also starving, and I order a plate of fries to eat right before I leave.

It's been a long day, and we all only leave the hospital around three in the afternoon.

When I get home I have to remove every inch of the clothing on my body in an attempt to cool off. The January weather is unbearably hot, and the combination of the heat with my hot flushes makes it necessary for me to lie on my bed naked, with the fan on its highest setting blowing in my direction.

I spend the next day mostly in bed attempting to distract myself from my nausea, mild headache and lethargy. When I first came across the terms "chemo brain" and "chemo head", I giggled because they sounded just like the infamous "preggie brain". The chemo version refers to how the effects of chemotherapy make it difficult to concentrate or think clearly, while also reducing one's memory. I have it, for sure – I can barely read a Twitter feed or a Facebook comment, let alone a magazine or a novel, and I feel completely listless and disinterested in everything.

I have been finding that whenever I feel ill from the side effects of chemotherapy, exercise has always done me a world of good. I eventually muster up the energy to get out of bed, and I start working out to a few simple exercises that I have already downloaded to my iPad. As always, moving my body is quite challenging initially, with me feeling like I'm about to vomit, but I feel so great afterwards that I'm glad I've done it.

I am also finding All-Bran Flakes with water to be my most edible breakfast – because I can't tolerate the taste milk leaves in my mouth, having it with water seems to prevent the nausea. I'm also managing to eat a lot of my own home-made lentil soup, which I store in plastic tubs in the freezer and which I can easily heat up whenever I am hungry and unable to cook myself a meal. When Thierry is home, he has been doing most of the cooking. He goes to work every day and touches base with me by telephone throughout the day. Depending on what time Zwelami needs to be collected from school, he also sometimes comes home to check on me again.

—•—

Six days before my next treatment, on a Thursday morning, I drop Zwelami at school for a music camp, which he is set to return from on Sunday. I have been tiring way too easily, I have been feeling light-headed and have had dizzy spells.

Little do I know that my immune system is trying to tell me something.

I have an appointment with Dr Demetriou in the morning, and a blood test reveals that my white blood cell count is down. She proceeds to give me the Neulastim booster again, in the hope that it will help. She also gives me a prescription for painkillers to ease the side effects of the booster.

—•—

Dr Demetriou has told me on several occasions that I need to monitor my temperature to check whether I am running a fever. I do not make that purchase until the next day.

I have been home all day feeling really sick. I have a dry and persistent cough and nasal congestion, and I decide to start wearing a mask again. It feels like my symptoms are getting worse as each hour passes. I soon have an excruciating headache and bone pain that throbs all over, in all my joints but especially in my spine. I feel like hell warmed up, and my body feels heavy as I lie on my black leather couch in the lounge, listlessly facing the TV. I'm not comfortable, so I struggle to get myself to walk upstairs to my bedroom.

I probably should have bought my painkillers immediately after receiving the prescription from Dr Demetriou, but I thought I could handle it because of my high pain threshold. I wanted as little as possible to do with painkillers. Trying to tolerate it proves futile, however, and the situation soon has Thierry rushing me to the chemist, where we purchase the painkillers along with a new digital thermometer.

Standing in the pharmacy, we open up the see-through cover and get a reading of 38.2°C. For a second afterwards, Thierry and I think the gadget is reading the outside air temperature because the day is so hot. A normal reading is 37.4°, so something is definitely wrong. Cautiously, Thierry says that we may need to go to hospital, but that we can probably wait and see what reading we get once we're back at home.

When I get home, I take my temperature again and then we take Thierry's as a comparison. My temperature of 39.5° has me calling Dr Demetriou's mobile number. She tells us to head to the Donald Gordon Medical Centre, where I am admitted on arrival.

At the same time as I am giving my details for admission, my blood is being drawn to check whether I have an infection. I discover that my blood pressure and sugar levels are down. It is afternoon, and for some reason I think I will be home by the evening. Then the nurse mentions that it will be a long stay, and I realise that I'm not about to be discharged anytime soon. This is the first time I will overnight at the centre; as it turns out, I will in fact spend the whole weekend here.

Throughout my stay in hospital I am attached to a drip through which I am given antibiotics because those I was taking at home were clearly not working. No matter how much pain medication I am given, I am constantly in serious pain.

I take a bite of my lunch and have to run to the bathroom to throw up. When I return to my bed, my grandmother

My Aunt Zenani and me at my grandfather's home in Qunu in our traditional Umbaqo attire for my brother Zondwa's traditional wedding in 2012.

My grandmother at a photo shoot we did.

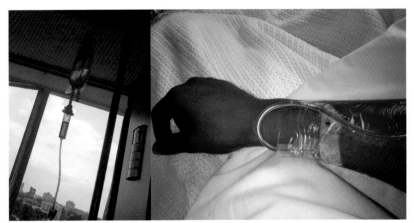

The appropriately named "red devil" or, "red death" – the reason behind my hair loss, mouth sores and all the other horrific side effects I encountered as a result.

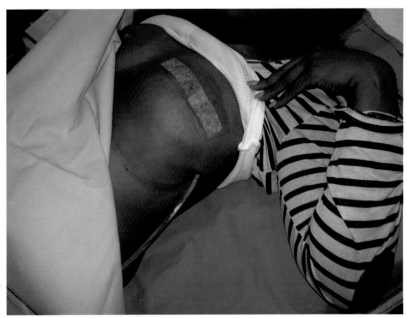

Having the tubes removed that had been inserted to drain the fluids I accumulated after my bilateral mastectomy in 2012.

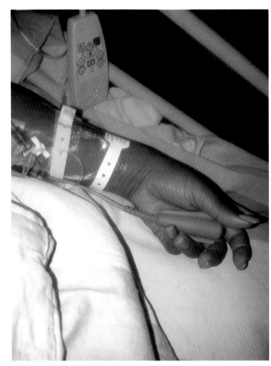

This is the morphine pump I woke up to after my bilateral mastectomy.

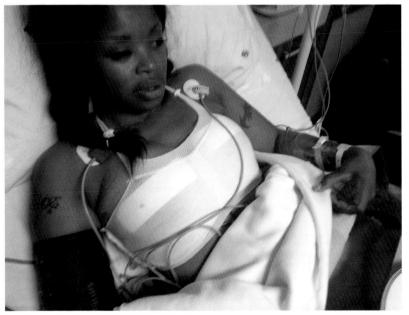

Immediately after my bilateral mastectomy in July of 2012. Looking like a HOT MESS.

Two weeks after my first chemotherapy treatment my hair was just falling out!

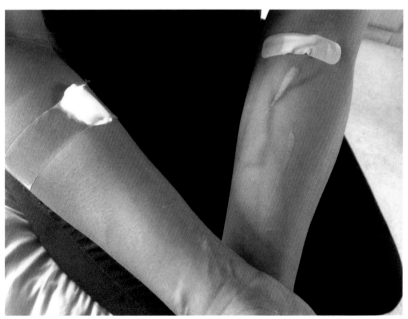

The dark lines are my dead veins caused by the chemotherapy – impossible to use and very painful and hard when touching them.

The cooler box I stored my fertility medication from Vitalab In Vitro Fertility (IVF) Clinic to keep out of the sun.

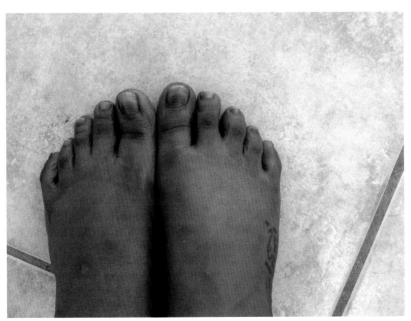

Another side effect of chemotherapy – changes to my fingernails and toenails; they always looked bruised and dirty.

The medical mask I had to wear to protect myself due to my weak immune system caused by the treatment.

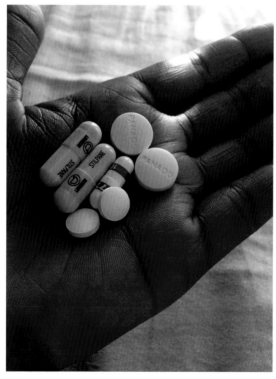

The amount of painkillers I had to be on for the bone pain and headaches, the side effects of Neulastim.

The chemotherapy caused puffiness to my face. I had hot flushes and bags underneath my eyes. (You can literally see the shape of my body on my linen.)

Zintle and Thatohatsi and me. These special ladies in my life shaved their hair in my honour and supported me at my treatments.

My partner Thierry and me attending the Rugby Festival at Saint Stithians College last year after my bilateral mastectomy.

My grandmother, my Aunt Zenani and Sis' Zodwa at one of my chemotherapy treatments

says that she saw how I was battling to get the fork into my mouth, fighting the urge to heave. I am given medication to prevent me from vomiting again and I feel more settled, although the headache remains.

On the second day, I am genuinely shocked to have my father pay me a visit, and I assume that my grandmother, my Aunt Zenani or my mother must have called him to alert him of my hospitalisation. I find myself in tears at the very sight of him.

Although my father and I had never had an argument, or even so much as exchanged a harsh word with each other, somehow around the time of my breast cancer diagnosis our relationship had taken a negative turn. After a lifetime of idolising him, when I came to that point in my life I no longer saw him as a man incapable of fault. To me, instead, he became a man who did not know how to be there emotionally for his own daughter. I felt rejected by him and my mother and so I'd created an impossible distance between them and me.

Now, with tears travelling down my cheeks, I get off my hospital bed and go and sit next to him on the arm of his chair. We haven't had a relationship for over a year now, and I cannot articulate the emotions I am feeling – even after he has left the room.

Early on Sunday morning, the doctor working in the ward tells me that I'll be discharged at midday as long as my temperature behaves itself and stabilises. Not long after that, Dr Demetriou comes to see me. She asks me how I'm feeling about going ahead with the next chemotherapy session, which is scheduled for three days' time – she feels strongly that we should give it another week because of the hospitalisation.

I agree. My body feels like it needs a hiatus, and I have cabin fever. I can't wait to get packing and get out of here.

I am discharged with just enough time to spare for me to go home for a quick shower and change – then I go fetch Zwelami, who is returning from his music camp at about four in the afternoon. It's funny how it's all miraculously worked out in the end, because it's as if the whole interlude was all part of a plan – I'm very relieved that Zwelami didn't have to visit me in hospital yet again.

———

On my last night in hospital I notice that I have what feels like a bleeding rash on the inside of my nostrils, which is quite painful and would last for close to two weeks. I'm not too sure what exactly caused it, but it may have been a result from the antibiotics I was on. Fortunately, the sores in my mouth have finally disappeared. My energy is seriously depleted and when I'm finally home again, I have to really psych myself up for my usual morning Zumba workout. But I persevere: I run up and down my stairs ten times and do fifty stomach crunches before completing my workout with a stretching routine that always leaves me more energetic.

My fifth chemotherapy treatment will now form the next phase of treatments, the first of twelve weekly sessions for the next few months. It's been postponed by a week and I try to make it as normal a week as possible.

Chapter 31

Fifth chemotherapy treatment (eleven to go)

AT QUARTER TO EIGHT ON 6 February, Thierry and I arrive once again at the Donald Gordon Medical Centre, and once again we are met at reception by Kim, who takes us upstairs. We are not in the room too long before a nurse from Lancet Laboratories comes in to take my blood for testing. But my veins are hiding today – I am being pricked by the needle, only for it to be removed and pricked again. In fact, everything feels like it is taking forever today: from awaiting the results from the blood tests, to receiving my grandmother and Aunt Zenani.

A little while later, Dr Demetriou walks in to tell me that my white blood cell count is high and so we may begin with chemo, which is always a relief to hear. We've had two postponements to the treatment so far, and although I understand why they have been necessary, I hate feeling that the end is moving further away from me.

Then Dr Demetriou tells me about the next few side effects I should expect: joint pain in a day or two; facial flushing the following day; watery eyes; a runny nose; a nose bleed; restless leg syndrome at night, which involves sensations of creeping inside the calves when sitting or lying down or an irresistible urge to move my legs; and breaking out in hives, which will be exasperated by exposure to the sun. Her main concern, she says, is the numbness I might experience in the tips of my fingers and toes. To protect the nails on my hands and feet, she will provide me with Elasto-Gel hypothermia gloves, which feel like they are made of pure ice.

So the worst is over, she tells me. It seems that from now on, as long as I don't have to deal with nausea, and a few of the "pesky" symptoms she has just described, then I can function like a normal person.

When she leaves, Octavia, the "vein whisperer", comes to prepare me for my chemotherapy and it's such a pleasure to see her again – it feels like she's an old friend. She tells me that the doctor has asked about my veins and whether they are still okay. She goes on to say that some people resort to having special ports implanted into their chests so that their blood stream is more easily accessed during chemotherapy. She must sense my concern, though, because she quickly tells me not worry about it, as there is no indication that I need a port. By the time she next comes into my room, I have been onto Google to see pictures and read up on the process, and I am watching a video of port-implant surgery. Dr Benn warned me about the dangers of taking to the internet as a means to self diagnose. The cyber world can be so unbearably deceiving – leaving you in despair and shock. I learn that when a patient's veins are difficult to access, port implants are placed underneath the skin of a patient's chest in order for them to receive intravenous medicines.

When I discuss it with her, Dr Demetriou voices her concern that if we opt for a port, I will have to undergo yet more surgery. In addition, because I am still young, she is worried that the implant could cause scarring; and there is also always the risk that I could wind up with a collapsed lung if it is accidentally punctured during surgery – carrying with it the risk of infection. I resolve to continue with the needles.

The weekly treatments that I am about to start will contain pretty much the same medication every time, which will be administered in the same order and in the same dose: A saline solution is given first, to keep the IV line open. Once that is finished, I will be given 1mg of Kytril, which is an anti-nausea medication. Then there is 12mg of Decadron, which is also used to prevent nausea and to reduce allergic-type reactions during chemotherapy, followed by 50mg of Zantac, which reduces the amount of acid produced by the stomach. We'll end with 6.25mg of Phenergan, which is an antihistamine also used to combat nausea, and which is notorious for its sedative effects.

And that's just to prepare for the chemo drug, Paclitaxel, which comes afterwards.

It is after I have been given the antihistamine that everything takes an unexpected turn. The nurse comes in to add 1410mg of Paclitaxel to my IV drip. She then tells me that she will indicate when I should put on the Elasto-

Gel hypothermia gloves that have been sitting on my table next to me. These ice-cold mittens will need to be placed on both my hands and my feet, and will remain there until the medication is finished. Dr Demetriou has said that, as it tends to get a bit cold – *no kidding!* – it will be okay to remove them if they started feeling too uncomfortable.

I am exhausted, and I attempt to keep the gloves on for as long as I can, although the more I try, the more exhausted I feel. The monitor keeps going off because of the way in which the drip has been inserted into my arm – the slightest movement disrupts the flow of the medicine, so I have nurses coming in literally every minute. But I still fall asleep for what I am told is a solid hour, and am later woken by the nurse removing my drip from my hand once the chemotherapy session is over. Even after that, I sleep for another thirty minutes.

As I am leaving, Dr Demetriou tells me that I should alert her if I find I have severe restless leg syndrome, in which case they will alter next week's dose. I must be really out of it, though, because one moment I am feeling all giddy, and laughing my head off, and then the next moment I'm dozing off again.

We only leave the hospital just before three, and even then I'm not awake for most of the journey as Thierry drives us home.

The effects of the antihistamine only wears off much later, shortly before midnight.

I hate the way I am feeling – it feels as if I have been smoking marijuana and am coming down from a major high. Instead of the paranoia and hallucinations, though,

I'm left exhausted and groggy. All I'm craving is soda, and I drink almost an entire bottle of Fanta Grape in an attempt to restore my depleted energy reserves.

And then I'm hit with the guilt. The guilt that comes with the realisation that I have, for a few minutes, enjoyed the illusion of the high as if it were some kind of escape. In an attempt to console myself, I send messages to two friends I was in rehab with to tell them how I'm feeling.

Chapter 32

Sixth chemotherapy treatment (ten to go)

MY SIXTH CHEMOTHERAPY treatment on Wednesday, 13 February comes in a week in which things are getting testy in my relationship with Thierry, which leads to us spending a night apart.

It also coincides with my Aunt Zenani's departure to Buenos Aires. She has been posted as South Africa's new ambassador to Argentina, and even though I've known that her departure is inevitable, it is still painful.

I have rescheduled my chemo for a later time in the day so that I can see my aunt off, and I call my grandmother to arrange for her to collect me on her way to the airport. The plan is to head to my chemotherapy treatment straight away afterwards. I have just dropped Zwelami off at school and I am making my way back home to wait for her when it hits me that with all the traffic on the highway, I am not going to make it to the airport on time, even if I attempt to drive myself. Somehow, in the midst of everything else, my grandmother and I have confused my aunt's departure time.

It turns out that my grandmother has to rush to the airport without me, just in time for her to bid my aunt farewell before she catches her flight. I quickly call my cousins to ask them to tell my aunt that I won't make it to say goodbye, and could they do it on my behalf as I can't bring myself to do it.

When I arrive home from Zwelami's school, I grab my hospital bag and get ready to leave. It's a bag that my aunt actually bought for Thierry, and which I use for everything I need during chemotherapy – my iPad, notebook, magazines and notepad, and anything else.

For the first time since this all started, I head to the centre alone.

In my room in the hospital, I settle in by ensuring that everything I need is well within reach. But I am feeling tearful and emotionally compromised – a feeling that will linger for hours. Here I am in my hospital bed with just my own company, and so upset that I haven't had the opportunity to say goodbye to my aunt like everyone else has.

And why does she have to leave at the time when I need her the most? The truth, I know, is that there would never be a good time for her to leave if I have anything to do with it. It has been a scary time anticipating her departure – not knowing how I will deal with her leaving. The thought has made me sick to my stomach.

I know that from now on the chemotherapy is going to be a reminder that my Aunt Zenani is no longer around, as she has been for so long – and at such a crucial time in my life. The previous Sunday my heart had tugged a little, knowing that she would not be joining Thierry and me again when we went to pay our weekly visit to Zenani and Zenawe at the cemetery.

When Dr Demetriou comes to see me, she asks me why I have arrived so much earlier than expected. I can't contain myself any longer and I sob as I try to explain to her the impact of my aunt's departure, although I know how positive this move is going to be for her. She asks whether I am closer to my Aunt Zenani than I am to my mother, and I respond by saying that she and my grandmother and Thierry have all been there for me from the day I was diagnosed, although I can't say the same of my mother – they have all remained consistent in their support. Unfortunately I don't have an existing relationship with my mother or father.

And it is true. My grandmother, my Aunt Zenani and Thierry are the foundation on which I have built my strength. With their encouragement and support, they are my relay team – they have held my hand and walked with me from the very beginning of my race to get well.

Dr Demetriou holds me close to her while gripping my hand and it is remarkably comforting to have her want to do that for me. That is what I appreciate so much about her and Dr Benn – their willingness to give of themselves so completely to ensure that my journey and those of others can be as smooth as possible.

Just as Dr Demetriou is leaving, my friend Zintle walks in to find me in tears, and it isn't a moment later that Thierry arrives with my grandmother. It had been such a rough week for me, and to have Thierry now sitting with me on my hospital bed makes a world of difference, despite my endless tears. Perched at the foot of my bed, my grandmother clearly feels so helpless and is blaming herself for the state that I'm in. Not knowing what else to do to stop my tears, at some point she phones my cousins to ask them to visit me in the hospital.

As the treatment begins, the nurse battles to find a vein and has to reinsert the needle a few times. On the fourth attempt, my vein is found by Octavia, who is quite a pro at locating them. The first nurse later comes back into my room to apologise, because she is under the impression that she is the cause of my tears.

As teary as I am, I burst out laughing and, for my own sanity, I convince her that she is not at fault. No one is.

I am asleep just minutes after the antihistamine is administered, and for the duration of the chemotherapy. By the time I get up, Thierry has my bag packed for home and we all leave after the drip is removed from my arm. Zintle takes my hand and holds it from the moment I walk through the door of my hospital room, because the medication has me feeling slightly dizzy and still so sleepy. We make our way downstairs, saying goodbye to my grandmother, who has used a different parking area.

As is the routine now, I eat the takeouts Thierry has bought me in the car, and on the way home we fetch Zwelami from school. Today I am dropped off before Thierry takes Zwelami to his extra Maths lesson. Like every Wednesday, when they come home, Thierry will organise dinner. It is hilarious how he now always ensures that there's a two-litre bottle of Fanta Grape in the fridge to quench my thirst.

We've put our disagreement behind us and I'm so glad he's back.

My grandmother has mentioned on several occasions that she feels there is a reason why I was not meant to bid farewell to my aunt that Wednesday – she thinks perhaps my immune system would have packed up as a result of all the emotion, preventing me from receiving chemotherapy that day. She has also refused to allow me to attend the funeral of my cousin's grandmother, because she says that she finds my immune system very unpredictable and scary: I can appear to be well, but I might actually be ill. She is worried all the time that I will put unnecessary strain on my immune system, and she is concerned about my emotional wellbeing.

If my grandmother is not worrying about my immune system, or me not eating enough, it's about how she thinks I need to seriously get help around the house. I can't recall how many times she has attempted to have someone assist me with my daily chores at home. She complains that I want to do everything myself and that I am obsessed with cleaning, forgetting that she accuses my Aunt Zenani and me of something everyone in the family knows is true of her. She makes me laugh.

It is true, though – I do everything around the house myself, because I have a system that I feel is only efficient if it is done my way. It works, too, because in the mornings, by the time Thierry and Zwelami are out of the shower and getting ready for school and work, the beds are made, breakfast is ready downstairs and their clothes for the day are ironed and waiting on their beds. It reminds me a lot about something I learnt at Houghton House: the importance of discipline and structure. It was my addiction counsellor who told me that I sometimes need to learn to ask for help. And back at the fertility clinic, Bernice helped me see that so much had transpired in my life over which I had little control, that I now tend to milk the opportunity to control anything. Call me a control freak of sorts, but I need and thrive on structure. I wake up between half past four and five o'clock every morning and jot down my agenda for the day in one of my notepads, and I take pride in knowing that ninety-nine per cent of my list will be actioned by the evening.

During chemotherapy, I am spending most of my time at home or running errands, except for when I'm in hospital. Apart from getting better, my number-one duty is to cater to my son and Thierry. I suppose I shouldn't be surprised, then, when I come across a piece of paper that Zwelami is working on for school. It is a speech about his family and it reads: "My mother is a housewife of Fourways." I beg him to remove that line from his speech, and he finally does so, but as much as Thierry and I are in stitches about it, it leaves me wondering just what my son thinks of me and my role in his life. If Mommy was working full time, who would attend every single sport's game he's ever participated in? Who would be parked an hour early in the school parking lot with an umbrella in hand when it's pouring outside, so that I can get him into the car without getting wet? Who would drive back and forth between home and school three to four times in one day because he has forgotten his sports kit? Who would be holding his hand at the dentist, or cooking his three meals a day?

There are benefits to spending so much time at home, because I am able to take care of him emotionally, but then not having an income from a job sometimes has him too embarrassed to bring friends home, because we live in a three-bedroom rental with a splash pool when most of his friends, so he says, live in mansions. Still, I don't think I would trade it. For the moment, doing this chemo, keeping on top of my home, loving Thierry and raising Zwelami are all I can manage.

Chapter 33

Seventh chemotherapy treatment (nine to go)

THIERRY AND I ARRIVE LATER than usual to find Zintle already waiting for us at the medical centre. I met Zintle through my Aunt Zenani – she is her lawyer – and have found we have a lot in common, including our love for my aunt. It is a relay team indeed – Zintle has taken the baton from my aunt, and is keeping an eye on me during my treatments.

By the time Thierry has to leave for a meeting, my grandmother has arrived, despite my brother Zodwa's wish for her to stay in bed. She has taken ill since her trip to the funeral I recently missed back home in Bizana, but I think she probably feels the need to be here for my chemotherapy, especially since my Aunt Zenani has left.

Last week's chemotherapy treatment barely gave me any of the side effects I had expected – I had none of the facial flushes, the numbness on the tips of my fingers and toes, and joint pain. That was such a relief and left me with so much less to worry about. If I experienced any joint pain, it was probably because I had attempted a high-impact workout as opposed to the moderate one I should have been doing.

So I am feeling optimistic. The Lancet nurse manages to find a vein on the first attempt, and within thirty minutes Dr Demetriou arrives with a nurse who mentions how well I am looking, and that I do not look like a patient at all. By the expression on Dr Demetriou's face, I can tell that she's relived that I appear to be doing much better than during our last encounter. I love hearing how proud she is of me.

The saline insertion buttons that are located underneath my breast expanders have become uncomfortable, especially if I'm required to bend over for long periods. I ask her when she feels it will be safe to have them replaced with the implants. She tells me that I will need to wait an entire month after my last chemotherapy treatment. There are so many factors to consider, but this is mostly because the chemotherapy will delay wound healing, and will affect my body's ability to fight infection. It will be better to first establish whether my cell counts have normalised, and whether I am in good medical condition before attempting the replacement surgery.

My grandmother watches me take down notes in my notepad, and tells me that she wishes she'd been as diligent a patient as I am. I know it's not just diligence: if I don't jot down all this information, then it's as good as not being told in the first place. I can't remember much if I don't write it down, and then I find I have to ask Thierry or whoever else was in the room when Dr Demetriou was talking to me.

Despite all the positive affirmation, I know that I've been feeling tired all week, and it isn't too much of a surprise when Octavia tells me that although my white blood cell count and immune system are not weak, my numbers are low and I should monitor them. This means that I must once again wear my surgical masks whenever I'm in contact with crowds, or anyone who may be sick. Also, gargling after every meal with the solution my oncologist recommended will be to my benefit.

——◆——

This time when Lancet draws blood from me, I have a bit of internal bleeding. It isn't anything to be alarmed by, and although it hurts, it looks more painful than it is. But it is unattractive, and it takes weeks for each bruise to clear up. Generally, the bruises have been impossible to hide because the February heat – made worse by my menopausal hot flushes – has left me wearing as little clothing as possible. If I am even slightly overdressed, sweat beads run down my face from the top of my scalp like someone has opened a tap. I attended a Narcotics Anonymous meeting at my home group in Benmore, and on one particular day I deliberately wore a long-sleeved top to hide the dark bruises left by my chemotherapy – my veins look so bad that I am really concerned that everyone will think I have begun shooting heroin. I know my truth, but I'm not going to take any chances. It is so important to me that everyone knows and sees how serious I am about my recovery.

This time, when my drip is inserted I have to be especially careful, because the drip is positioned near my elbow joint – any movement will slow down the process of it getting into my system. My Aunt Zenani calls me all the way from

Argentina just moments before sedation creeps in, and I am ecstatic to hear the sound of her voice on the other end. This is about to become the norm: we will speak on the phone every Wednesday afternoon, making it feel as if she is right there with me, and not on the other side of the world.

As unbearable as the cold gloves are, each session I stick it out for as long as I can. My grandmother tells me that I unconsciously remove them and then return to my induced sleep, and it's always funny when she imitates how rebellious I seem when I take them off – clearly just wanting to continue snoozing! I've been onto Google and read how some patients put on thick cotton gloves and socks beforehand, which allows them to have their feet and hands in the mittens for longer periods before it gets too uncomfortable. It seems like a good idea.

Today, I wake up when the drip is removed and find myself still so fagged by the time we reach home. I feel slightly more energised after drinking out of my two-litre bottle of Fanta Grape, and it isn't too long before I've managed to tidy up the house, and I even wash the dishes after dinner. Thierry feels I might as well eat a cup of sugar at the rate at which I'm drinking the soda, and has asked that we find a substitute for my sugar craving.

Better yet, does he want to switch places with me so we can see how *he* handles the side effects of chemotherapy?

I am always amazed at how refreshed I feel the morning after my chemotherapy. Now that we've switched to the weekly treatments, I am no longer experiencing that debilitating nausea. My "morning after" almost always begins with a workout, and I am quite convinced that continuing this throughout my treatments has had a positive impact on me. I know that when I get good exercise in, especially in the mornings, it pretty much sets me up for the day. I try not to beat myself up too much on the days that I am too exhausted to work out, and I find other ways to make up for it.

And as much as I sometimes might like it to, normal life does not stop for chemo. My landlady requested that I have a few painters and plumbers at my place, and they have been repainting walls and repairing the plumbing for over two weeks now. I have been in contact with them quite a lot of the time as they work around the house, bringing them water or a two-litre bottle of whatever colddrink I've managed to buy, preparing sandwiches and bringing chocolates and snacks for them to eat at my glass table on the patio outside. At times I wear my surgical mask. But to be honest, I don't always wear it, because I'm more worried that they'll think I'm being funny towards them.

Two days after my seventh chemotherapy treatment, I am back in hospital again – only this time I am taking care of my grandmother, who has been admitted to the same medical centre for the weekend. Thierry, Zwelami and I had actually intended to spend the weekend with her in Soweto, and spending that time with her in the context of a hospital pains me. I hate seeing her this way. Earlier, I called to tell her that I was running late in getting to Orlando West. Over the phone she deliberately gave me the impression that she was in hospital for blood tests and was just waiting to go home. It was Sis' Zodwa who confirmed that she is actually in a bad state. In less than an hour, I am next to her hospital bed weeping my eyes out at seeing her asleep and looking so vulnerable.

It is only when Thierry pulls me aside behind the hospital curtain that I stop crying. He places his hands on my shoulders, telling me that although it is difficult not to cry with everything that is happening, I need to hold back my tears for my grandmother's sake: it will do her more harm than good to see me crying. He says I should try to be strong for her.

"Don't let her see you crying!"

I wipe away my last tears and compose myself before she opens her eyes and finds me with her.

Back in the day, my grandmother and I used to devour pies voraciously and she always used to say that a pie would never be wasted if the two of us were around, because I would only eat the pastry while she would only eat the meat. It was our "thing". This story comes back to me as I look at her, and I think about how often she has been here, in this hospital, for me. Now it is my turn to be there for her. Looking after each other is our thing.

I spend the entire weekend at her beck and call, and it gives me some satisfaction knowing that I am being useful rather than just sitting at home. Instead the nurses have wheeled in a bed for me right next to her so I can look after my grandmother.

When she is discharged two days later, the stress of having her there is at least alleviated, although not exonerated altogether. I don't realise how exhausted and emotionally drained I am by the experience until I get home.

———◆———

When Sis' Zodwa mentions that my grandmother's blood pressure shoots up each time I am hospitalised, it breaks my heart into a million pieces. Now is the time I should be looking after her, but instead I'm stressing her out with my cancer. Just like I'm stressing out my aunt, my grandmother, Thierry and Zwelami. My cancer has had a huge impact on their lives; as the ones who are sick, we tend to forget that our loved ones go through it too.

My week hits a more positive note when Thierry arrives home to surprise me with a new external hard drive he's bought me. The laptop I have been using as a journal to detail my journey with breast cancer has packed up, and someone from Hewlett Packard has confirmed that fixing it will cost the same as buying a new laptop.

I can't afford a new laptop for now, so Thierry shares his with me. For the longest time, and at every opportunity he gets, he has been pestering me to write. He's always stressing how I need to get onto his laptop to continue writing because he believes it is important that I share my experience.

The external drive is symbolic – it is a place of my own to store this evolving story of mine.

Chapter 34

Eighth chemotherapy treatment (eight to go)

ONE HUNDRED AND EIGHTEEN days after first being diagnosed with breast cancer, I reach my halfway mark: there are just another eight treatments until I am done with chemotherapy.

I am emotional at the realisation that neither my grandmother nor my Aunt Zenani will be walking over the threshold of my hospital room this morning; I contain my tears and soon dry my eyes at the thought that I am actually never alone, especially since I have both Zintle and Thierry in the room with me today.

It must have been a lucky day as my veins are found by the Lancet nurse and Octavia on the first attempt. Dr Demetriou visits briefly, leaving after telling me how happy she is with the effect the treatment has had on me this far.

This time I have made sure that I packed some thick cotton socks and gloves to bring with me. Wearing them ensures I am at least able to keep my hands and feet in the hypothermic mittens for as long as I can. I only remove them when I go to relieve myself in the bathroom and wash my hands – while it is a good idea to drink plenty of water to flush out the chemotherapy medication, I make endless, laborious trips to the bathroom, which interferes with my sleep.

When I get into the car to head home, Thierry places on my lap a box of the most delicious grilled prawns and fries. I eat it en route to fetch Zwelami from school, and then I doze off again while still in the car.

I wake up shortly after arriving home and shock not only myself but also Thierry and Zwelami when I am out of bed and in my kitchen cooking dinner that very night.

My nails and hair are growing so quickly that I have to cut them at least every week or two. Although my feet are still much darker than the rest of my body, my hands are slowly getting their ordinary colour back. My urinary tract infection flares up every now and then, but it is nothing I need antibiotics for any more – drinking plenty of water and the occasional Citro-Soda eases any burning discomfort.

In the mirror, I watch as Thierry and Zwelami play with what I like to call my "chemo hair": I do not regard the regrowth of hair on my head as mine, because it feels and looks nothing like the hair I had before chemotherapy.

Anyway, it seems to keep them amused.

Chapter 35

Ninth chemotherapy treatment (seven to go)

I'M SITTING IN THE CAR IN the parking lot at the medical centre, and I'm telling Thierry how absolutely bored I have become with chemotherapy. As I slowly near my last treatment, it feels like being in the last trimester of pregnancy – I have to try convince myself that I'm almost done.

———

I am over the moon when Dr Demetriou arrives before Lancet, informing me that I won't need blood tests before my chemotherapy this time. My grandmother arrives impeccably on time, just as Octavia puts in my drip. Thierry orders me the biggest chicken burger known to mushroom sauce, which I eat during the antihistamine drip. For some reason he feels that the chemotherapy has fewer negative side effects if it gets to me on a full stomach, so he has been bringing me a meal from the café downstairs. Sometimes I feel like I've eaten cement afterwards, especially because I fall sleep immediately after the meal, but I always enjoy it nonetheless.

Fortunately, I haven't struggled with the metallic taste after the cocktail of drugs that is so commonly experienced by chemotherapy patients. They say no two people are the same, and I've been lucky enough never to have had to find tricks to disguise the sudden foul taste of the food I put in my mouth.

By the time I get off the phone to my Aunt Zenani, I am pretty much ready for the sedation to take effect. Although I am as exhausted as usual, I don't sleep through it as much as I have before.

—•—

Five days after my ninth chemotherapy treatment, 11 March marks my thirty-one months of sobriety – an unforgettable milestone for me. The highlight of my week is driving to my home in Soweto, where I meet a filmographer and photographer sent to capture a few images and sound bites for the United Nations' Global Road Safety Week, an event called the "Long Short Walk" for the Decade of Action for Road Safety, the goal of which is to prevent five million road traffic deaths by the year 2020. The initiative is supported by the Zenani Mandela Campaign, which is raising awareness of the current outrageous death toll suffered by our children.

At Zenani's school, this week my family and I are

joined by her friends and former classmates, and I have the opportunity of leading the walk in memory of my daughter and every single child who has lost their life due to road accidents.

My heart is heavy as I look into the crowds and notice some of her closest friends. Hearing them speak about what they loved and miss most about Zenani takes me right back to the moment when I realised that she was never coming back. I will never get to apologise for missing her thirteen birthday.

I wonder what she would have looked like today, but it doesn't matter how many times I hope to spot her there among her friends – I can't see my baby.

Chapter 36

Tenth chemotherapy treatment (six to go)

DR DEMETRIOU MENTIONED week that she would be attending a conference abroad during the week of my tenth treatment, and that another doctor would be standing in for her while she was away. Because of her absence, it is once again important to have Lancet come and get a blood sample before my chemotherapy treatment.

Then Dr Wadee walks into the room and asks whether I am all right with him consulting with me. I'm fine with the arrangement, although Thierry looks extremely uncomfortable as the doctor checks the state of my breasts. I remember a story from when I was first diagnosed, about a woman who had undergone chemotherapy and reconstructive breast surgery. After talking about her journey, the woman would almost automatically lift her shirt to expose her breasts – an act that required no thought. Similarly, when this doctor walks in and asks to examine my breasts, the top and bra I am wearing quickly come off, and I have absolutely no inhibitions. It's strange, but I have become so used to this change in the concept of my personal space.

My cousins arrive unexpectedly and I am both shocked and happy to see them walk into the room. By the time my grandmother arrives, I am yet to receive my treatment as there has been a delay with the arrival of the medication. My cousin-in-law keeps asking if I am really undergoing chemo, which makes me laugh. It reminds me of how, during the first few treatments, my Aunt Zenani told me that I didn't look like I had just had chemotherapy because I had driven myself to her place, while she expected me to be bedridden and ill. I have had the pleasure of hearing so many people make reference to how my positive attitude has influenced my treatment, and how well I look as a result.

Generally, I have been feeling great and I know that it has a whole lot to do with the good choices I make to feel better about myself.

On Friday morning, on one of my twice-weekly visits, I walk into my grandfather's bedroom and I am almost reduced to tears when he smiles, extends his hand to hold mine, and puckers his lips for a kiss. At these times, I always sit with one hand touching his, more amazed than the last time at how soft and warm his hands always are. We don't have to exchange words, but we feel each other's affection and that to me is more than I could ever ask for.

As I leave my grandfather's place, one of the policemen posted in the security room walks up to me. He tells me he thinks I am so down to earth, and he thinks that's why I'm such a beautiful person – not for what I look like on the outside, he says, but for who I am on the inside. I am so touched by his words. It is a reality check to have someone say something so unexpected, and he'll never know how much these words mean to me right now.

My experience with addiction, cancer and life has taught me so much. I have been humbled in so many ways, and I feel I have learnt to differentiate between what matters most to me and what matters little, and how to better nurture the precious things in my life. When I left rehab two-and-a-half years ago, what I feared most was being unable to stop myself from using. I knew I never wanted to live like that again, but more importantly I knew how much hurt, disappointment, anger and shame I had brought to my loved ones. I wondered then how long it would take me to repair that colossal damage – if it was possible at all.

I am still filled with intense guilt and remorse.

I am still unable to forgive myself, as some of my family has begun to do.

I can only hope that with each day that I live a sober life, I give all three of my children a reason to be proud of the mother I am now becoming, because nothing devastates me more than not being the mother that Zenani deserved. I failed her, and I live with that reality every single day.

I still have nights where I'm up in the early hours of the morning, unable to sleep, thinking of her, what happened and what I could have done to prevent her from losing her life.

Chapter 37

Eleventh chemotherapy treatment (five to go)

THE 15 MARCH 2013 MARKS a year since my official diagnosis. This week, as I face my eleventh chemotherapy treatment, I think of all that has come to pass since that day.

As much as I reflect on my cancer "anniversary", I don't celebrate it. In fact, for some reason I have struggled to recall the precise date of my diagnosis by Dr Benn – a detail that I blame on "chemo brain". All I have is the month and year on my tattoo, and so I have to call her rooms to fill in the rest.

At home, while we are preparing ourselves for our excursion to the medical centre, Thierry asks me an unexpected question.

"Baby, how do you feel when you hear of someone actually losing their battle with cancer …? I've never asked you that before."

I cringe.

Survivor's guilt?

To be honest, when that happens, it feels like I'm the sole survivor of a plane crash and it would be difficult to explain the guilt or the heaviness in my heart that comes with receiving the news that someone else has lost their battle with cancer. It is hard to believe that not so long ago, I was quite adamant about refusing treatment and would have felt more comfortable having the cancer spread through my entire body until it was finished. I had thought that trying to fight cancer would be far worse than trying to live with it.

Little did I know.

———

Days are now leading quickly to the end of my chemotherapy treatments, and I am as emotional about its end as I was about its beginning.

How can something I never wanted now be something I am attached to? My chemotherapy sessions have become a lifestyle in a way, almost automatic in their routine. Anyone would think I would be bursting at the seams with absolute joy as I near the end, but I am miserable and depressed about it.

What happens now? What will I do every Wednesday? And do I spend the rest of my life waiting for that fateful day when Dr Demetriou tells me that despite six months of chemotherapy treatments the cancer has come back? That it's found a place in my body where they are not able to operate?

Would I agree to chemotherapy for a second time if the disease returned?

"I hate it when you talk like that," Thierry says to me each time I tell him that we need to prepare ourselves for the eventuality of the cancer coming back.

"See, baby," I say whenever I hear of someone who is battling cancer for the second time, or who has succumbed to it. "Hers came back, even more aggressively. My cancer's definitely coming back. No one is ever that lucky, baby."

But the idea scares me more than he can ever know.

———

For the time being, on this Wednesday I have a new nurse from the centre, and she is administering a muscle-strength test on me. I appreciate protocol, but it comes as a funny surprise – after all the treatments I have had every week for almost six months, this is a first.

The nurse from Lancet Laboratories proceeds for the second time to locate a vein to draw blood for the routine test. When she's done, she looks at me and asks if the hospital nurses open a new file for me each time I arrive for chemotherapy. When I tell her they do, she bursts out laughing at the idea that this is the eleventh time I will be asked the same routine questions in the same order.

Of course, some answers are more revealing of my mood than others.

"Are you pregnant?" a nurse will ask.

Wouldn't that be amazing ...?

"Not just yet, but ask Thierry and me in a few months, please?" I might reply.

Not too long after the nurse from Lancet leaves, Dr Demetriou arrives and asks everyone to clear the room so that she can examine my breasts. After I've removed my shirt and bra, she begins feeling them for any bumps. While she does so, I notice that the nurse who is with her is standing right behind her, facing the other way as if she is hiding. The nurse may be giving me my privacy, but she looks very awkward, and I suddenly become conscious of my bare breasts. It has been so many months since my bilateral mastectomy that I've almost forgot that I have no nipples, let alone breast tissue – Thierry reminded me one night when he told me he remembers exactly where they were, and what my own breasts used to looked like.

To be honest, I do not miss my natural breasts or nipples as much as I thought I would, although it still pains me to think that I will no longer have the luxury of breastfeeding a baby or producing milk. I will never share that very intimate moment when a baby suckles to its heart's content.

Will this make me less of a mother to my future baby?

I have been feeling swollen and puffy and, as I expected, Dr Demetriou confirms that I have been retaining water. My ankles are naturally thick (thanks to my grandfather) but my left one is always the first to swell up when I am retaining water, and it seems to worsen when I don't drink enough water or work out as much as I should. I have always found that strange: how you solve water retention by simply drinking more water.

I've been too tired to attempt any form of exercise, so it's been slightly over a week and Dr Demetriou suggests I try again.

Today, I am treated to gifts from Thierry and Thatohatsi, who is just as persistent about my health as my other supporters are. I get flowers from Thierry, and a jewellery box with the breast cancer emblem on it from Thatohatsi. Their thoughtfulness has me smiling for hours on end as I feel so special and cared for. Once again I am reminded of the remarkable support I have received from my family and friends. I can't imagine how I would have been able to walk this journey without them.

As he always does, Thierry makes the trip to the café downstairs to find a meal which he feels will sustain me. Just as soon as Octavia finds my vein (on the first attempt), I am attached to a drip and ready for the chemotherapy medication. Before the sedation takes effect, I eat my meal and then deliberately refrain from drinking more water than my bladder can handle.

I am rewarded when I doze off having made far fewer of those disruptive trips to the bathroom. My grandmother says I get my weak bladder from her.

After the treatments I am always hungry, and thirsty for something really sweet. When I get home this time, I have a little more energy in me than the last time: just enough to remain on the couch downstairs waiting for Thierry to bring home dinner.

When he gets back, he pleads with me to go upstairs to the bedroom to sleep, but I manage to watch TV without dozing off all the time.

Two days after the treatment I am at my son's soccer tournament running after my niece and nephew. Thierry and I have had the pleasure of babysitting them while their parents are away at a wedding. I've seen how amazing Thierry is with the kids, and I can imagine what a wonderful father he would be.

We spend the weekend with my grandmother at her home in Soweto, and I couldn't chose for a better way for it to end than for us to be sitting at her dining table sharing a meal that she has cooked herself, especially for us.

Chapter 38

Twelfth chemotherapy treatment (four to go)

THIERRY AND I ARRIVE very late – eleven thirty, as opposed to the usual quarter to eight. I am unnerved about the time, even though I indicated to Dr Demetriou the day before that we would be late.

When we arrive, she gets everyone to clear the room so that she can examine me, and I am thoroughly relieved when she says I don't have to get my bloods done. We have a brief chat about my anxiety over nearing the end of my treatments. I still can't imagine what will become of this particular day of the week – stopping chemo has left a gigantic question mark hanging over my Wednesdays.

I realise that my chemotherapy treatments entail so much

more than the administration of the medication. Whenever I arrive at the centre, I am guaranteed to be surrounded by my loved ones; I've always looked forward to seeing Dr Demetriou walk into my hospital room with a registered nurse; I've enjoyed interacting with the other on-duty nurses. I have even made a point of experiencing each of my chemotherapy treatments in its entirety, no matter its outcome.

Now, I feel as if I am leaving the nest.

———•—•———

Soon after Dr Demetriou leaves the room, it dawns on me that if I am to remain on hormone blockers, it will be difficult to fall pregnant. She has said that I am to receive these shots every three months, which obviously means that I am in the infertility run for the long haul.

My heart sinks and I turn to Thierry.

"You may leave me if you want to. At this point I can't give you any more babies and who knows if I'll ever be able to conceive," I say.

"Baby, don't be silly," he replies. "I'm not going anywhere.'

Meantime, Octavia has to find an alternative vein after the needle bends as it's penetrating my arm, but it isn't anything too painful. Zintle hands me the phone to speak to my Aunt Zenani, before I eat a lunch of steamed vegetables that I prepared the night before and have brought from home. Thierry's never had to force a meal down my throat because I can never refuse food, but I have been feeling the need for something lighter, and today there is no way I am going to be inhaling whatever greasy meal he chooses from the café. I seem to have put on quite a lot of weight this time around.

I doze off after the antihistamine finds its way into my system, and then awake to find Thatohatsi and Zintle on either side of me putting on my cotton gloves and socks, before stuffing my hands and feet into my dark blue cold mittens. Everything is happening in slow motion and although I think I am awake, it feels like I am sleeping. Sometimes in my sleep I hear the conversations around me, although my eyelids are too heavy to lift and see who is speaking.

Even though I doze off again immediately, soon I am laughing in my drug-induced sleep. Lying on my hospital bed, I must be a sight to see – I'm sure I look like a dead fly on its back with four legs in the air, or a sheep or cow after it's been slaughtered, with the men holding up its legs to be skinned.

The nurse wakes me up as she is removing the drip a while later, and I open my eyes to see my son Zwelami sitting to the left of my bed, eating the lasagna Thierry has bought from the café downstairs. He looks so comfortable sitting there, listening to grown-folks' business, exactly like Zenani used to do.

I am so happy that he waited until he was good and ready before deciding to join us at these chemo sessions. A few months ago, when he was on school holiday, I begged him to come and experience a treatment with me, but back then he refused very quickly. Both he and Thierry can't stand needles. I've asked Zwelami whether he feared coming to see me that first time I received chemo in hospital. He says he didn't at all, because he knew what to expect. Like he expects that I will be sleeping in the car when we collect him from school after my treatment; and he knows that when we arrive home I am always tired and will soon be found sleeping on my bed.

This routine is part of the reality these days – and it is amazing how children just come to accept it.

———

When we were talking in the hospital room, Dr Demetriou said that I should remain positive, but when I arrive home a little later, I am in tears.

What I'm finding so daunting is not the pressure that will come with the new chemotherapy-free chapter of my life, but more that I feel I have to bid farewell to a part of my life that I want to prolong. For selfish reasons, I am just not ready to end my treatments or wrap my head around having to replace my Wednesdays with something else.

What does life after cancer and chemo mean, anyway?

I am still so exhausted that after I've nodded off, I sleep an hour or two longer than usual, and I am woken by Zwelami entering my room. He wants to show me a photo of Thierry as a child, carrying his sports trophies – Zwelami has put the picture in an empty frame of his and now places it near my bed (although soon it will migrate to his own bedside, in a new frame, taking pride of place just above his Play Station games).

Thierry and Zwelami share such a special bond and I adore how invested Thierry is in my son's life. Zwelami loves the picture of Thierry as a school boy holding his most prized trophies because Zwelami is a sports fanatic himself. Up until now, I don't think my son has believed all the stories Thierry has told him about his sporting successes, but Zwelami now has proof! I love how Thierry has felt the need to share this part of his life with Zwelami – even though, at times, his stories are awfully exaggerated!

Thierry is cooking when I tell him that I will not be eating dinner. He brings it upstairs to my bedroom anyway, and serves it to me on a tray. The man seems to know me better than I know myself, because I eat everything on the plate, not having realised how hungry I am. Afraid that my bladder will keep me up all night, I stop myself from drinking the whole two-litre bottle of Fanta Grape that he's also thoughtfully brought up with my meal. When we were in hospital today, he had Thatohatsi in stitches over how much I eat – but then he complains that I don't eat enough! It's hysterical when he relates this to her, because it's so true: on the evening of a chemotherapy session, I have an appetite bigger than Thierry's, Zwelami's and my usual one put together! Boy, can I eat.

After dinner, Thierry, Zwelami and I all lie on my bed for a little while, watching television. Then I rouse myself and manage to tidy Zwelami's room and hang out his school uniform and then I hang out the rest of the wet laundry to dry. I've exerted myself, and the activity exhausts me enough that I need to go back to bed to rest.

I call my grandmother to check that she's okay. I noticed that she had been very quiet all through my treatment. She tells me she was actually very worried about me during this last session – I had lost my balance leaving the bathroom as I made my way back to my hospital bed. She says she can't figure out whether it is the fatigue or the medication that is causing it. Also, it concerns her that my Aunt Zenani is not around, because my grandmother says she would not know how to cope if I am ever hospitalised again.

But as it turns out, it's not me who is hospitalised.

When news breaks out that my grandfather is in hospital once again, I am in an emotional quagmire. I feel trapped.

Normally, I am the kind of person who takes to Facebook or BBM to share what is going on in my life, good or bad. Having to remain absolutely silent about his condition has me ignoring even my closest of friends – and I am petrified about what every new day means for his health. When he is back home, I find myself driving over to Houghton to spend some time with him – and more importantly, to see for myself that he is indeed all right.

As a teenager my grandfather used to drive me insane with the type of birthday present he always gave: books on various countries across the globe. If we were lucky enough to get money from him, there were always two conditions attached: give a detailed explanation on how the money was going to be spent, and provide a receipt as proof that we'd spent the money on what we'd claimed we needed it for. As kids growing up, we had to watch the news and he was always drilling the importance of education to us: "Darling; I want you to get your first degree here at home in South Africa and once you're through with that, I will pay for whatever college you choose to go to in America." As it happened, he and my mother had ultimately refused to let me leave for college in 2000 after being accepted at the University of Pennsylvania, and they'd had their reasons. But, while I don't regret not leaving to study abroad, I do regret not documenting the trip I took with my grandfather in the Presidential jet to Morocco in 1994 when I was fourteen years old. I remember the stopover we made in Nigeria on the return trip to fill up the aircraft; in the airport, I walked into what would have been the State Protocol Lounge to see my grandfather sitting with the Nigerian president and various other statesmen.

I wish I'd made entries in my diary about the many conversations we had which I no longer recall, or taken pictures of him showing me how to wave to the public as you flash your teeth and nod. I remember how he always needed to know where I was and who I was with, and how, when I was eating dinner with him during that trip, I had to taste everything on the table like he did out of courtesy.

Out of the flood of memories about my grandfather, the only thing I distinctly remember him saying to me is: "Darling, one day you're going to follow in my footsteps." He's never expressed it, but I know that over the years since that state visit I have shamed, disappointed and hurt him and my family.

"*Utshata nini?*" he asked me in 2005 at my Aunt Makaziwe's home as my cousins and I stood at the door, waiting to join the procession during my Uncle Makgatho's funeral. There was no hello – just a pause to question me on when I was getting married – before he left with a hearty smile.

During my visits to him these days we sit in silence. But that's okay – to me, just his presence is enough.

On Saturday, Thierry and I collect my niece and nephew from my grandmother's place so that we can attend a school rugby festival – only to realise that we've got the date wrong. It gives me the opportunity to spend a bit more time with them at my place. But, Murphy's Law, the evening sees me running late for a remembrance service at the Bryanston Methodist Church, a church introduced to me by my Aunt Zenani. It is a memorial service for all families who have lost loved ones, and I have been feeling quite strongly that I want to attend, along with Thierry and the kids.

At the church, candles are being lit in memory of our departed loved ones, and the woman who is assisting hands me a single candle. I ask if I can light two candles – for both my son and my daughter who have passed away – and I find myself failing to hide my tears. I try to stay composed because of my little niece, whose hand I am holding. After Zwelami and I have lit our two candles we make our way back to our seats, where for the rest of the service I sob quietly while my niece sits on my lap.

Even today I am in disbelief at my loss. Will I never get to hold Zenani or Zenawe in my arms again?

————•————

I have a feeling that Zenani and Zenawe are around me. One morning at the cemetery I walked up to the tap to fill my garden water containers when a young boy walking with his mother pointed to my left.

"Look, Mom – there's an angel." I know for a fact he had seen Zenani.

If I didn't know it before, I knew it then: I am walking with two angels on either side of me now.

Now, in everything I do, in the places I go to and the things that I see, I always wonder how it would feel to have Zenani and Zenawe with me. I told Zenani that she should start driving when she turned sixteen because she would need to start taking her brother to school – little knowing that she would never see that day. My heart aches when I get lost in fantasies – I can almost picture her and Zenawe playing together with Zwelami – only to be reminded that my babies are now my ancestors who I pray to.

My babies, whom my heart and womb still ache for to this day.

If only lighting a candle could help me find my way through the darkness to them.

Chapter 39

Thirteenth chemotherapy treatment (three to go)

IT HAS RAINED ALL NIGHT, and the rain has continued this morning. As usual, Thierry and I arrive at the centre after having dropped Zwelami off at school. Kim meets us at reception again, and once we're upstairs, a nurse starts walking us to a room. She asks which room we would prefer, which has Thierry picking the one he feels is most spacious. A different nurse introduces herself and lets me know that she will be handling the admission form today, and taking care of me for this treatment. It isn't too long before another nurse checks my blood pressure, sugar levels and temperature, which are all fine. And then Zintle arrives.

So far, so normal.

While we go through the motions, though, I can't help but think of how I've been given a second chance. These past few months of chemotherapy and the recent changes have given me a new perspective on my life. I know it is time to get my priorities in place and to start planning the next phase.

Dr Demetriou herself is starting to look ahead to my chemo-free life. She tells me today that normally I would be on hormone blockers for a duration of five years, but that she is willing to compromise on that because she knows exactly what it is that I want. She gives me a smile that would give any rainbow a run for its money.

Zintle knows how desperate I am to try for a baby as soon as the chemotherapy is complete, and doesn't hesitate in reminding me that waiting two years will make me at least thirty-five by the time I can hypothetically carry a new pregnancy. She tries to make me understand how much more complex this whole process is becoming – to make her point, she leaves her seat and the work she has been doing on her laptop, and comes to stand at my hospital bed. I can't help but laugh as I hear her voice reach its highest octave, and I appreciate her point.

But for me it is very simple: I want to have another baby, seven more if I am lucky enough.

Before Dr Demetriou leaves, she says that she is excited about us reaching the end of the treatment and that I should not ruin my last chemo experience by worrying about what is to come. She reminds me to live in the moment, enjoy the accomplishment of finishing treatments, and then worry about other things once I am done with chemotherapy.

So I surrender to the now-familiar process, reflecting on how far I have come.

I am glad once again that I do not have to have Lancet draw blood from me. Yet another nurse comes to attach the drip to my arm, but as soon as she has penetrated the skin, my arm swells up with the needle still inside. Zintle and I can't believe the sight of the huge swollen arm of mine – we're both shocked, and then repulsed, and Thierry pretends not to see a thing, scared as he is of needles. The nurse has to remove the needle and makes another attempt on the back of my hand, which is all the more excruciating because she tries to chase a hiding vein. A nurse I haven't seen before arrives to assist – she locates the vein much quicker, although my arm nearly blows up again.

Chemotherapy number thirteen finally commences and I am hoping that this time I won't have to experience the nastiness of the nosebleeds I have been subjected to recently.

By the time the Phenergan is administered, I have polished off the lunch that Thierry has bought me. For some reason, although I sometimes slip into a drug-induced sleep, I am awake for most of the session, and can open and close my eyelids when I feel like it, without having to force them open.

Thierry and Zintle take turns replacing the cold mittens on my hands and feet. When I do fall asleep, I tend to remove them, but I also show no resistance to having them put back on. When I'm awake, I keep turning my head to the left to check the drip. It usually takes up to an hour to finish the Paclitaxel, and when I notice that there is no more liquid in the clear bottle hanging just above my head, I know that I am finally finished today's treatment. It has seemed slightly longer this time because I have been more awake and thus more conscious of it.

By the time I get to the car I am feeling a whole lot better and I manage to stay awake the entire car journey. On our way home after collecting Zwelami from school, we all get out of the car to purchase a milk tart from the Fruit & Veg City just a few blocks from my place.

When we get home, I stay sitting downstairs on the couch and watch TV. Thierry cooks dinner while I help myself to two very large portions of the milk tart.

———◆———

A friend of mine once jokingly advised that I write a book about how I made cancer look good. She was left in stitches when I showed her how my lace wigs tend to slide backwards to the middle of my scalp, and how sometimes I only realise it's happened when people's attention suddenly shifts from my face to the top of my head. I told her, like I tell anyone, that I am an "illusionist" – that every photo I ever take, whether it is of a plate of food or shots of myself, goes through a tedious process of elimination and editing to fit my personal standard. Zintle laughed when I showed her how I Photoshop my pictures of the meals I make for Thierry and Zwelami before posting them on BBM or Facebook – who does that, anyway?

When I look at the many photographs I take on an almost daily basis, I can see why she and so many others mention that I don't look like I've had cancer, or a bilateral mastectomy, or that I've undergone six months of chemotherapy. But a girl must have a plan, and this is mine: concealer to hide the dark rings under my eyes, a lace wig to hide my weak, protein-deficient hair, nail varnish to hide the darkening of my nails, and eye shadow mascara to hide my very thin eyebrows and eyelashes.

What these generous souls don't see are the number

of times I've looked less turned out. Like the time I was getting ready to leave the house to go out with Thierry: I had grabbed my handbag off one of the chairs in the dining room and was making my way through the kitchen to the garage when he looked back at me and said, "Baby, you left your hair." I had to go back to the dining room to get it, laughing as I carelessly put it on my head and then adjusted it. I walked to the car wondering just how my day would have turned out had I left my wig at home.

When I'm at home, I never really wear my wig – one of the first things I do when I walk into the house is toss my wig aside, or place it on a wooden towel rack in the bedroom. Especially when I feel a hot flush coming – it makes my entire scalp and face perspire.

There are very many unglamorous moments, of course. Every other night, I am woken up by my drenched sheets – one of the chemotherapy medications produces the symptoms of menopause and, like me, many patients experience severe hot flushes that literally soak sleepwear and sheets. One time, I turned on the bedroom light and even took a photograph showing how my night sweats – or nocturnal hyperhidrosis – had produced the detailed contours of a figure on my sheet. I have found the most uncomfortable part of this experience is the chills that accompany the night sweats, and which have me shifting over to the warmth on Thierry's side of the bed.

During the day, I do feel that some of my hot flushes are triggered by certain situations that make me flustered – such as a long queue at a shopping centre. Once, I was growing impatient standing waiting to pay for a few items I was buying for one of my brothers – and I could literally feel my scalp glistening underneath my lace wig. Beads of sweat that had been collecting on my scalp starting dripping down my face to meet those forming on my cheeks, before racing down towards my cleavage. Zwelami, who was standing next to me, turned to look at me and said at the top of his voice, "Mom, you're hot flushing!"

These days, it doesn't help me much to rush when I am getting dressed to go out – all it does is cause me to sweat so much that I have to stop and sit with my bedroom fan blowing onto my face for ten minutes before I eventually cool off. My grandmother gave me two beautiful Chinese fans which I use if I can feel a hot flush coming on – which seems to be happening more often now than it did in the beginning. I love using these fans, because they solve the problem with a sense of sophistication.

So, of course, while I do take lots of photos, there are still many moments that don't make it onto my camera.

Looking good has so much to do with how I feel on the inside. Even make-up doesn't make up for the fact that I have had the most amazing support structure – from my medical team to my beloved friends and family, with each and every person carrying the baton in this relay race with me. I feel like they have made a winner out of me, and I will always, sincerely, be indebted to them for that.

I have come to appreciate the many different things in my life that make me feel good.

Another two of those things are my small furry sons, Thizo and Benzeey, who, ever since I adopted them, have not been aware of the fact that they are actually canines. I think that has a lot to do with the fact that they both slept on my bed as pups, and literally travelled with me everywhere I went in the comfort of a handbag.

I really do feel that both my pets have such healing

qualities, and these days I still love spending time with them, whether it is taking them for a walk to a nearby park or around the neighbourhood, playing with them or watching a movie with them (even though they, like Thierry, tend to doze off five minutes into it). At any given time at home, whether I am inside or outside, Benzeey will remain by my feet while Thizo will be getting up to mischief. I always refer to them as my furry sons because at the end of the day they do behave like kids, and they are so dear to me.

"No, I am not your friend. I am not friends with dogs," my grandmother always says to them when they run up to her in excitement.

When Benzeey and Thizo wore black-and-white outfits that matched a jersey of mine in public, my grandmother could have fainted.

"Darling, that can't be normal."

How we laugh!

Chapter 40

Fourteenth chemotherapy treatment (two to go)

MY FOURTEENTH CHEMOTHERAPY treatment on 10 April follows the day after my thirty-third birthday, the highlight of which is dinner with my friends and family. Sitting not too far from me at the dinner table is my Aunt Zenani, who has flown home on business. My grandmother brings a gift to where I am sitting – a new bicycle – and I squeal like a little girl receiving her first bike. I am *so* excited – my grandmother knows that I have been wanting to take up cycling now that I am almost done with chemotherapy and soon won't need to stick to only moderate exercising. I enjoy challenging myself, and due to my biopsy I had to stop the boxing I'd loved after only three months. After the reconstruction, I'd been more worried about my new breasts than my face, but before that I had briefly considered taking up boxing professionally – although my grandmother, my brothers, Thierry and my trainer at the time had all laughed at me.

Step aside, Laila Ali ... Okay, maybe not.

My grandmother and Thierry ask that I only ride my new bicycle in the complex, because they feel it is much safer there. I am instantly reminded of how, when I used to walk my furry son, Benzeey the Jack Russell, Thierry had insisted on driving next to us to ensure our safekeeping. Quite hilarious considering I had been walking Benzeey long before I ventured into a relationship with Thierry, but I've learnt to appreciate how overprotective he can get, given the unusual circumstances he's been introduced to ever since he's known me.

Since my diagnosis and the onset of chemotherapy, I feel like I've lived in a glass house under the watchful eyes of my loved ones. I'm in my early thirties, and my grandmother will still call me to say, "Darling, please dress warmly – it's cold outside today."

I think when you are very sick, they fuss over you so much because they were worried they were going to lose you.

———

This morning, en route to the medical centre, Thierry and I stop over at the nearest Woolies Engen garage to purchase mushroom and cheese burgers, with dessert, for breakfast. Back in the car, he breaks into a song he has composed, which he calls "Hiroshima has got nothing on my baby". He sometimes tells me how at my birth I must have come out of my mother's womb saying, "I *said*: I. Don't. Want. To. Come. Out!"

I admit that I have become snippier and more irritable of late. Since the chemo started, I have often been moody and anyone has had the potential to get on my nerves. It's normal, I'm told – all just side effects of the chemotherapy, and Thierry doesn't always know who he's coming home to. But weighing in on Thierry's obvious concerns about me is the worry that I disclose so much about myself, our relationship and everything to do with my cancer to almost everyone. He wants us to keep something of our story to ourselves. Naturally, I have to respect that because my journey with cancer involves so much of him, and it is a priority of mine to ensure that he is comfortable with my process. It's a tricky one.

When we arrive at the medical centre, Kim meets us at reception with a huge smile. All the medical staff wish me a happy birthday, as does Dr Demetriou and almost every medic I'm in contact with. It is just after eight thirty, and Thierry and I proceed to the fourth floor so that my sugar level, blood and blood pressure can be tested.

When Dr Demetriou arrives with Octavia for my checkup, we have a quick chat about an email I have sent to her and Dr Benn. I have decided that I want to volunteer at a facility that caters specifically to cancer and chemotherapy patients. Knowing I've been worried about the future of my Wednesdays after chemotherapy, at a previous session Dr Demetriou suggested that I go out for breakfast or a spa treatment on those days. I've given it some thought, but I am more attracted to the idea of somehow affiliating myself with organisations needing volunteers to assist with their patients. At this point, in my own mind, I am more than prepared to mop floors, clean up vomit or serve tea to staff and patients to take up the time between eight and three o'clock every Wednesday.

When I mention this to Dr Demetriou, she says I wouldn't necessarily have to do all that, and she goes on to enlighten me about a few other issues I have neglected to consider. I appreciate how she feels I will need to nurture myself for a month or two before I can give back to others. And she says that some time off will give me the opportunity to consider what exactly I want to do, bearing in mind that she also has a few concerns about my recovery. Naturally, Thierry agrees with her as he also believes I need to take time to recuperate – he knows from experience that I don't always know when I am tired. But he also knows that, obstinate as I can be, this will make more sense to me if I hear it from Dr Demetriou herself.

Once she is done with the checkup, she tells me that after getting to know me, she is not surprised that I want to volunteer. I feel immediately warmed by her sentiments.

Moments after Dr Demetriou leaves my room, Kim walks in to present me with a birthday card and hamper from the centre and staff. It is filled with all sorts of goodies – including all kinds of things to help counteract nausea from the chemotherapy. I'm so touched by the thoughtful gift, and we chat for a while. I tear up when Kim says that they need me to feel like I am one of them. I know that I absolutely do – so much so that the medical centre has begun to feel like home away from home.

Octavia, my vein whisperer, prepares me for chemotherapy by attaching me to a drip, finding my vein with ease on her first attempt. This time I don't have to have Lancet come in to draw my blood, and I don't have to be pricked and prodded more than three times in a single day. Despite the tea and juice we receive from the kitchen staff, Thierry takes a walk to the café to buy Zintle and me hot chocolate, and then he has to leave for work. Zintle then leaves her laptop on my bed so I can listen to her music while she goes to check up on another friend of hers who has been admitted for cancer treatment to the same medical centre.

Not long afterwards, my grandmother walks in dressed up in the most beautiful traditional regalia. She's thought to pass by en route to an event with the president, though she can't stay for long. It is right after my Phenergan dose, the antihistamine which always has me sleeping within minutes. She laughs when I tell her I'll see her on the flip side – on cue, we both realise that the medication has started to have its effect on me.

The next time I open my eyes, Zintle is pulling my bed linen to one side so she can put on my cotton gloves and socks. I notice that she doesn't place cold mittens on my feet any more – instead, I'm wearing cold slippers made especially for feet. She tells me that it isn't the first time I've used them, and that I was so out of it last week that I hadn't noticed.

Zintle has been such a good friend to me, and I am continually astounded by her care. She pays attention to every detail: the frequency with which the drip runs into my veins, and anything else that happens on each day of chemo. Sometimes I have to ask her about details so that I can jot them down in my notebook. I found it hilarious when I saw her getting a crash course on how to monitor the drip from one of the nurses. She stays so up-beat: every other second she breaks into song, and she's forever asking the exact questions I will need answered by the time I have left the hospital.

This part of her reminds me so much of my Aunt Zenani, who also always seems to ask the right questions of the medical team.

My aunt has been attending meetings ever since she arrived back in Johannesburg, and so I don't expect her to make it to my fourteenth chemotherapy treatment. Having her here at home for a few weeks is more than enough, even though we chat almost every day on WhatsApp when she is away.

Zintle asks me whether she should buy me a burger from the café downstairs as Thierry always does, but instead I reach for one of the sandwiches laid out not too far from my bed, and within minutes of eating it I have drifted off.

I wake up as Zintle is calling one of the male nurses to inform him that the chemotherapy medication, the last for the day, is finished. She goes to drop off a few magazines for her friend and soon afterwards we are making our way to the car. As I'm getting in, Thierry calls to tell me that he will be waiting for me at home, and asks what would I like for lunch.

Soon after Zintle has dropped me off I am sprawled on the living-room couch making a video journal entry on my iPad as I usually do. After eating the lunch that Thierry has bought for me – which includes my two-litre Fanta Grape – I fight sleep for as long as I can, sitting up and changing positions so that I don't get comfortable enough to doze off again. But by the time Thierry and Zwelami return from his club soccer practice, I am asleep.

I rouse myself to eat two of the chocolate bars from the hamper that the centre prepared for my birthday, but I am still hungry and I wolf down the dinner Thierry cooks for me. He tells me that next time it will do me good to have a really big meal before the antihistamine, because I recover much quicker – he says the Woolies burger and dessert I had a for breakfast don't count. We sit on the couch together and watch a movie while I eat, and I'm amazed at how energised

I feel immediately afterwards – suddenly I'm in the kitchen washing dishes, washing and hanging the laundry out to dry, and reading through Zwelami's school report in preparation for tomorrow's parent-teacher interview.

I have done a lot this evening, but I am exhausted by the time I called it a night, and I don't get a chance to reply to the email Dr Benn has sent in response to me wanting to volunteer. I'm thrilled to read, though, about how proud she is of me and how she would love to have a chat so we can come up with some ideas about how I can get involved with breast cancer awareness.

I wake up in the morning feeling strangely tired, still but manage to get some writing done after breakfast and to prepare for a few meetings I have during the course of the day. And then I do the cardio workout which I do every morning.

My hope is that my story will touch lives. I hope that it shows that no matter what family you come from and no matter who you are, experiences like mine can happen to anyone.

A few days after this chemotherapy treatment, while we are on our way to attend one of Zwelami's school and athletics activities, Thierry tells me a story about hope:

"There was a group of rebels and in that group there was a soldier who was a devoted Christian. Every day before he went into battle he would say a prayer, although his colleagues laughed at him, asking whether God listened to him and if he did, then why were there so many killings in

234

the world? This would happen every day, and the soldier never missed a day of prayer before a battle, despite the deliberate taunting he received. One day his captain asked him whether God really listened to him. The captain then said he would put the soldier's faith and his God to the test – if he failed, he would be forced to take his own life. The captain then called all the other rebels to come and observe what was taking place, telling them how he was going to put the soldier's God to the test.

"The captain and the other rebels knew that the soldier could not drive. They gave him the keys to an old car, asking him to pray for God to help him. The captain then said that soldier must move the car twenty metres from where it was parked. The soldier went down on his knees to pray, as everyone around him laughed. He got into the car and started it. He drove the car the twenty metres as he had been asked. By the time the car stopped, everyone else was crying. As he got out of the car, they all got onto their knees and said that they all wanted to pray to his God. The soldier asked why they were all so stunned, to which the captain responded that there was no engine in the car, and that the soldier's belief in God had moved a battery-less car twenty metres."

I love this inspiring story – it makes me feel that anything is possible.

One of my grandfather's quotes is also a huge inspiration to me. It reads: "The greatest glory of living lies not in never falling, but in rising every time we fall."

I find that in those times when I don't believe in myself, I only need to look at my loved ones to remind myself that no matter what I have been through, there is always a little bit more strength in me ... and a huge amount of Hope!

Chapter 41

Fifteenth chemotherapy treatment (one to go)

WEDNESDAY 17 APRIL 2013 sees my second last treatment.

Before heading to the medical centre, we have to drop Zwelami off at his aunt's place. It is school holidays and he doesn't want to join us for my fifteenth chemotherapy. Because we often don't have enough time to eat breakfast at home on Wednesday mornings, it has become the norm to pick it up en route to the centre, so after leaving Zwelami, Thierry and I drive to McDonald's to buy our breakfast of burgers, fries and soda.

We arrive an hour later than usual, and so we don't see Kim at the reception. We make our way upstairs and are taken to a new room not too far from the nurse's station in a wing of the hospital I'm not familiar with.

Unusually, the attending nurses arrive as a pair, but I assume it is because we are in a different wing. They are swift in their mission to test my blood pressure, blood sugar and temperature, which are normal, as expected. Dr Demetriou leaves me in a pickle when she walks in to find me literally stuffing my face with a quarter pounder with cheese.

"That's a not-so-healthy breakfast," she says, and I laughingly blame it on Thierry, though in reality I seldom refuse any food he gives me. He deserves it, though, because this morning he said, "So this is what a beautiful ET looks like," when I showed him one of my many photos of my almost bald head.

There is a different mood in the room today – a lightness, perhaps, and maybe relief. I seem to have processed both my fear of the chemo, and my fear of stopping it. I can hardly believe that after today there will be just one more treatment to go.

I am consumed with laughter when Dr Demetriou jokingly says she'll be getting her hair done for next week's treatment, and then tells the nurse who has walked in with her that the other nurses on duty next week should all wear make-up.

She then lifts my armpits to check the state of my lymph nodes.

———

I have had the idea for a while now that I would like to document my final chemotherapy session on film. I'm thinking it could then be part of a documentary that takes the shape of a journal of my journey with breast cancer, from diagnosis to post-chemotherapy treatment, using the video journals I've been making. Perhaps there will be some interest in the documentary once it is finished.

When I spoke to Claude, a family friend who has worked with my grandmother and my mother on a few of their projects, he was enthusiastic – going so far as to create a mock-up trailer just weeks after we talked about it.

Since it involves the hospital, I need to pass the idea by Kim, who comes up to my hospital room to chat about it. She believes the only issue will be, obviously, to maintain the privacy of the other patients who are there at the time of the filming.

It's exciting to see the idea start to take shape, and I feel very inspired as I contemplate sharing my story in this way.

———— ·•· ————

But for now, it's back to the practicalities of getting through this session. Our sandwiches, tea and juice are wheeled into the room on a four-levelled tray from the centre's kitchen. Octavia arrives holding the instruments she requires to set up my drip. I have asked my grandmother and Zintle to record her prepping me for the drip, which they do, having arranged themselves comfortably around my hospital bed. Playing her part perfectly, Octavia finds my vein on the first attempt, and then my grandmother resumes reading her papers and Zintle turns back to working on her laptop.

By the time the antihistamine is administered, Thierry has placed a beef burger on my bed tray next to my notebook, BlackBerry and iPad. I tell him I'm not hungry, but he says it will make him happy if I eat. My grandmother looks at him and then at me and tells me to please just eat the burger as I'm already feeling the effects of the Phenergan. I am high and sleepy while I devour my burger. Then I eat the

KitKat Thierry bought me in case I needed something sweet. Octavia has already placed my box with my cold mittens next to the tray with the snacks and refreshments, and while Thierry monitors the machine that pumps the medication into my bloodstream, Zintle begins helping me with my cotton gloves and socks before putting on the cold mittens and slippers. I soon doze off.

———

I wake up to Thierry taking pictures of me sleeping. I try to fight the exhaustion, but I doze off again. When I next wake up, it is to realise that the bottle of Paclitaxel is nowhere near finished, and I reach for my BlackBerry for a change.

By the time the nurse removes the drip from my arm, we are all very ready to leave. Thierry is shocked at how much energy I have when I don't require any assistance to walk from my hospital room all the way downstairs to the car. He says that I'm literally pulling him in my eagerness to leave.

In preparation for Zwelami's upcoming holiday to Argentina, where he will be visiting my Aunt Zenani for two weeks, we have to pass by the Consulate General in Sandton. There, I manage to fill out all the required documentation and we then proceed to the shops to do some grocery shopping. Back at home, Thierry cooks dinner for us once again and I'm able to wash the dirty dishes, fold up the clean laundry, get in some much needed writing time and watch television. I don't doze off at any point.

———

On Friday evening Thierry and I are sitting on the couch in the lounge with Benzeey and Thizo, watching a movie.

Over the weeks of chemo, the intense heat of summer has given way to autumn and now winter, and it is very cold this evening.

Today I paid my grandfather a visit in Houghton, as I have always done on Mondays and Fridays, and then I met up with my grandmother to do some shopping in Killarney Mall. It was while we were in a queue to pay that I had noticed a picture of my mother on the front cover of a magazine. And there was my name, just below her picture. My mother, I realise, has discussed my breast cancer with the media and I am gutted because surely she knows how much this will upset me. We're not on speaking terms, and haven't been for close to a year, but I still feel she should have at least cleared it with me first. In a rather juvenile manner, I turn the magazine the wrong way round to hide the picture.

All my life, my mother and I have struggled to find common ground. For years I blamed her for the physical and sexual abuse I was subjected to as a child – my feeling was that if she had been there for me, she could have prevented it and I could have been protected. The reality of the situation is that after I was born, my mother had had to resume her studies and she was also heavily invested in an all-consuming political life. She is a strong woman who was living in difficult times, and I have come to realise that she probably did the best she could.

Just at the moment, though, I've had my hands rather full with getting through this chemo and my life without her support, so establishing a more healthy relationship with her has not been a priority for me.

Without even reading the article, what has upset me is the fact that I didn't feel my mother has any right to mention my breast cancer publically, given that she hardly knows anything about my journey. Over six months, my mother has only been to one of my sixteen chemotherapy treatments. And I feel that she should at least have the courtesy of asking my permission before discussing my diagnosis with the media. Although I have never kept my cancer, my addiction or my children's passing a secret, and have shared so much about it on social networks, it is still *my* story to tell, and not hers or anyone else's. I am baffled that she would deliberately hurt me like this, and at such an unfortunate time.

———•———

It takes what feels like ages to finally make my way home after my excursions, and I am in a state after the incident with the magazine: for most of the evening I go from fighting tears, to crying them, to wiping them away, only to find myself yelling at the top of my voice as I tell Thierry about it.

We have eventually settled down to watch a movie, but as the evening wears on I am really finding it freezing. I plug in an electric heater and place it near my feet to keep warm. I must doze off because Thierry wakes me to say that we should make our way upstairs to bed, and so I get up. On the way, I pop in to the kitchen and grab something out of the fridge to quench my thirst.

I am pouring some soda into a glass when I feel incredibly dizzy.

I lose consciousness.

Thierry tells me that he was upstairs when he suddenly thought something might be wrong. He raced to the kitchen just seconds before I fell, and caught me before I reached the floor, narrowly avoiding knocking my head on the kitchen table.

What was that about my knight in shining armour come to save the day once again?

On impulse he places me in a sitting position, where he holds me for several minutes before I come to.

He gives me some water from my pink water bottle, and it is only after he asks me why we are sitting on the cold kitchen floor that it hits me what has happened.

Trust Thierry to arrive unexpectedly on time, once again! He seems to think my fainting has everything to do with how stressed I have been about my mother today, although I think perhaps I shouldn't have been sitting quite so close to the gas heater.

Thierry has me send Dr Demetriou a text to inform her of my fainting, and she advises that I drink plenty of liquids and keep her updated. If I faint again, she will need to have me admitted to hospital for observation.

———•◦•———

It rains all of Friday night and Saturday morning. When I wake up around six, I am too exhausted to work out as I normally do and I stay in bed longer than usual.

It is only on Sunday morning, four days after the chemotherapy, that I experience a tingling sensation on the very tips of my fingers and my two big toes. My fingers have been feeling sensitive but not unbearable for over a week, but now I feel a prickly pain on top of my nailbeds and down the sides of my fingers and toes. The best way to describe the feeling is as though they have gone numb after holding them against ice for too long. Thierry advises me to cut all my nails, which has helped, but removing my battery from my phone, cleaning my ears with my facecloth in the shower, rubbing Benzeey and Thizo's thick, furry coats, zipping up my boots, opening a can of soda or anything that requires the use of my nails is really beginning to hurt.

The nose bleeds, which are caused by low platelet levels in the body, haven't stopped altogether but are more bearable. It has come to be expected that each time I blow my nose I will find traces of blood on the tissue, and I can always feel the blood trying to push itself to the edge of my nostrils. These symptoms would be alarming if Dr Demetriou had not indicated that I should expect them.

Hopefully they will soon be a distant memory: my final date with chemotherapy is around the corner.

Chapter 42

Sixteenth chemotherapy treatment
MY LAST DATE WITH chemotherapy!

On the morning of my sixteenth and final chemotherapy treatment, Thierry and I have no need to wake up very early, as Zwelami is still on holiday in Argentina. However, Claude and his crew are scheduled to arrive at 6:45 to install a GoPro "action" camera on the inside of my car windscreen, which will capture footage of Thierry and me as we make our way to the oncology centre. After leaving home, we make a quick stop at a McDonald's Drive-thru for breakfast – thankfully the GoPro camera is only activated once we have received our food.

Every other kilometre or so, Claude and his crew pull

up next to our car to get some footage of us. To prevent Dr Demetriou making another comment about my unhealthy breakfast, I hog down my Egg McMuffin en route.

We arrive at the medical centre and soon the camera crew are dancing around us in an attempt to get the most suitable angles and images. Kim is there to greet us, and leads us out of the reception area. On the fourth floor we are brought to a hospital room we have used in the past, and where I will receive my final chemotherapy session today.

As we settle in, the nurses check my vitals and I sign various papers and verbally answer questions while a nurse fills out my final admission form. The Lancet nurse draws a blood sample, filling three vials after a second attempt at locating a vein.

Dr Demetriou arrives, looking as beautiful as ever, and we have a brief chat about what I can expect after my last treatment: she will have me on various maintenance medications, and I will need to come in to see her in about a month's time.

By the time the medication arrives, my grandmother, Thatohatsi and Zintle are all there, and my brother, Zondwa, my sister-in-law, Nondzolo, and Sis' Zodwa are on their way. Octavia locates a vein in my left arm in preparation for the saline solution, and nurses bustle in and out of a room that is rapidly filling with family and friends, as well as the camera crew, who are busily at work. With all the noise and excitement, it is easy to forget that I now have cameras following my every move, and I forget about the speaker that has been placed on my hospital bed to the right of my shoulder.

I eat Thierry's beef burger without protest and drink a can of my staple Fanta Grape, and then I begin to feel the effects of the antihistamine.

By the time Zintle has assisted me with the cold mittens, I am quivering with cold, and the nurse has to bring me an additional two blankets. Although I have tended to feel chilly recently – though this is interrupted by my many hot flushes – I have never experienced such a sensation of coldness like I do on this, my last day.

I doze off, then wake up to use the bathroom, and manage to fall asleep again before being woken by a phone call from my Aunt Zenani all the way from Argentina. I'm feeling sedated but still quite functional as I chat to her, and then participate in the other conversations going on in the room. Octavia then walks in to show me the results of today's blood tests, which indicate that my immune system is slightly down – this explains yesterday's fatigue. Fortunately, last week I took a picture of the paper with my blood results and it is still on my BlackBerry – Zintle and I find it interesting to compare today's results with last week's.

At some point I look towards my right to see how much of the contents of the Paclitaxel is left in the IV pump. There is still quite a lot to go, so I ask the nurse to increase the frequency from 100 to 150ml per hour, hoping that it won't burn as much as it usually does. At the moment, although the increased rate causes some discomfort, I just can't take what feels like watching paint dry for the millionth time. I take a couple of pictures as the last drops descend through the bottle, and as soon as the nurse removes the needle from my arm it finally hits me:

This is the very last chemotherapy treatment I will hopefully ever receive.

The funny thing is that for a second just before it ended, I regretted asking the nurse to increase the IV pump's frequency. I wonder if I should have savoured that moment for just a little bit longer.

Perhaps I should do something different to commemorate my last transfusion, but all I can do is make my way to the bathroom and cry out of sight of everyone. I try to compose myself before I walk back into the room, but it is futile.

As I prepare to leave, I hug every one of the nursing staff, and I thank them for everything they have done for me, which makes me cry even more.

I deliberately don't look back at the room as I make my way out.

—◆—

I am not as energetic and alert as I thought I would be, and I'm asleep when we drive through the main gate to the complex where I live. Once inside the house, I can only make it as far as the couch in the lounge, where I watch TV before falling asleep.

I'm later woken up by Thierry, who arrives with the two-litre bottle of Fanta Grape and crisps I asked for. Feeling drugged, I fall back into a deep sleep, and I don't hear Thierry trying to wake me up to give me the plate of food he has prepared for my dinner. It's only much later that I eat, and then I go upstairs to sleep.

I toss and turn all night, feeling incredibly hot, which then triggers more hot flushes.

—◆—

By the next day, as tired as I am, I am also feeling bored being at home.

I wonder what on earth "taking a month off" after chemotherapy to "pamper myself" will entail, because as far as I'm concerned, sitting at home watching television all day is simply not an option.

By the afternoon, I am already out shopping with my grandmother, after having a late lunch. Thierry and I also manage to work out together for an hour and a half, which we haven't done in a while, and which I enjoy immensely – I haven't exercised in over two weeks.

As it turns out, it will be a solid month after my last chemotherapy treatment before I resume a full work-out regime, because I still have to build up enough energy to trade my DSTV remote and Box Office for a pair of sneakers and Spandex. But there is a compelling reason to carry on: the chemotherapy medications have caused fluid retention and weight gain, a fact that I am reminded of when I look at my inflated ankles and the new fullness and roundness of my face. The good news is that I notice that the symptoms of water retention are alleviated when I work out, and I've also found that it helps for me to reduce my salt intake, increase my water intake and to keep on top of it by weighing myself daily.

———•—•———

Despite these distractions, during Dr Demetriou's proposed "month off", I grow even more lethargic, and I tire of the company of my symptoms on the days I am alone in the house. Purchasing the vitamin B-complex pills recommended by my oncologist is an attempt to alleviate the pain and discomfort I am still experiencing on my finger- and toenails, and the sensitivity around my fingertips. I have difficulty cracking an egg, using my BlackBerry keypad to text or dial a number, washing dishes, grasping objects with my hands, wearing certain shoes – basically, anything that involves contact with the nails on my fingers and toes.

If anything, the bruising on my nails has darkened, not lightened, and a few of them have lifted from my nailbed.

I have become very well acquainted with a strange feeling of warmness on the very tip of my nose, which is always indicative of a nose bleed. Every morning I have woken up with a slightly congested nose, which has any tissue I blew into covered in blood. It's not until the third week into my month off that my daily nosebleeds eventually dissipate.

We all respond to chemotherapy differently. As Thierry is my witness, I have made a note in my diary of every single change I have experienced, felt or seen on my body since my breast cancer diagnosis – to the point where he has sometimes called me paranoid. In my diary, throughout the process of chemotherapy, I have also written countless lists of the symptoms or side effects I could potentially experience, in case of a memory lapse (which I've often had). I've done this for numerous reasons, but mostly because I haven't been able to trust my "chemo brain": chemotherapy drugs do damage to the hippocampus, which is a part of the brain involved in the retention of memory, and I have struggled to access my short-term memory.

Nevertheless, doing this has helped me remember the kinds of details that I can reflect upon with fondness and amusement. Like how, inspired by a hot flush – or "power surge", as it is described on a little sign about menopause that Zintle bought me for my thirty-third birthday – I made a trip to a wig store in downtown Johannesburg. It was there that I picked a wig with the shortest hair possible, but one which at least had a fringe to conceal my non-existent eyebrows. By then, I also barely had any eyelashes attached to my eyelids, which shocked Thierry on the afternoon that I brought it to his attention. I remember how we laughed when I wondered aloud where my eyelashes and eyebrows had ventured off to. He replied that they must have run off to the same place as my pubic hair, after they'd decided to fall off and find solace in the toilet.

I also remember how my grandmother couldn't stop herself from laughing when I informed her that, at thirty-three years old, my pubic hair is now grey, an effect of the chemotherapy on hair follicles.

"Darling," she asked me, "what were you doing there to notice it in the first place?"

I have my first follow-up consultation with Dr Demetriou on 20 May 2013, just less than a month after my last chemo. This time, for the first time in six months, I walk into the Wits Donald Gordon Medical Centre on a Monday and not a Wednesday.

I have a bit of time to kill and am reading a magazine in the reception area when I hear the now familiar voice of my oncologist as she calls my name. She leads me to her office and then gives me the opportunity to voice any queries or concerns I have post chemo.

There is one overriding concern I have, and she knows exactly what it is. She goes on to explain that the chemotherapy reduces the body's levels of various hormones so as to shrink cancerous tumours and increase life expectancy. Of course, this has a bearing on my desire to fall pregnant, because we will need to wait between three and six months to see whether my ovaries will "wake up" on their own. It has only been a month, but I am already growing anxious as I have not yet experienced a menstrual cycle, which indicates a healthy reproductive system.

I sit in Dr Demetrious's office taking notes like a diligent patient once again, knowing I will need to pay close attention to the changes in my body caused by the post-chemo medications. Tamoxifen is a hormonal therapy which blocks oestrogen and prevents certain types of breast cancer – I am advised to take one tablet every day for the duration of five years, along with a Disprin, which prevents blot clotting in the legs (what is known as deep vein thrombosis). To add to my shopping list of warnings, I hear that Tamoxifen heightens menopausal symptoms such as hot flushing and night fevers, also causing very dry skin, thickening of the lining of the womb and mood swings, among other things. Vagifem is a vaginally inserted tablet prescribed to deal with the vaginal symptoms of menopause which I will use once a week to make sex more bearable for me.

Would it be too much to ask for my ovaries to kick back into health on their own so that I am able to conceive – even if it is only in two years' time? Dr Demetriou does not mince her words. She tells me about the harmful effects the Tamoxifen would have on my baby should I fall pregnant while I am still taking this medication, and insists that we agree to wait for a period of twenty-four months before taking a gap during which I can try for a baby. Cancer cannot spread to a foetus if a woman becomes pregnant while having the disease, but the medication she is taking for the cancer can harm the baby, especially in the first trimester of pregnancy, and can result in birth defects or miscarriage.

There are some problems with the plan – as I have come to expect, nothing is foolproof. I am meant to take Tamoxifen for five years, and I am fast approaching my mid-thirties. There are two competing priorities here: my health, and my desire to have a baby. Taking a pill every day for the duration of five years is said to halve the risk of the cancer returning in most young women. The small white Tamoxifen tablet is a very sensitive drug and, much like the contraceptive pill, it is more effective if taken at the same time every day. If you forget to take a Tamoxifen pill, you need to take it as soon as you remember – in other words, it's not the kind of thing you mess around with. But I will have to interrupt this programme if I hope to conceive again – in fact, once I am off the drug, I will have to wait for a period of six whole weeks before even trying to fall pregnant, and then I cannot take it for the duration of the pregnancy. How long after the birth of a baby will I have to revert to taking it again, I wonder, and is there a window period I will need to observe before trying for another baby? There is clearly a lot to consider, and only time will tell what the next chapter looks like.

After all that information, it's a great relief to hear the relatively simple news from Dr Demetriou that my breast reconstruction can begin as soon as I have been cleared of cancer.

As our appointment winds down, I'm advised to return for another checkup in three months' time, during which I will have a menopausal scan to check my oestrogen levels and a blood test to check my cell count, because chemotherapy reduces the number of white blood cells.

But the highlight of my session with Dr Demetriou is one that marks the very pinnacle of my journey with cancer, and the transition into the next phase of my life: I am given a clean bill of health.

I am officially cancer free!

Epilogue

My new crop of "chemo hair" is curly and wavy for the most part, and is more of a lighter shade of brown than black. It resembles that of a newborn baby. When my hair fell out, it started at the back of my head, and it hasn't grow back uniformly either, a fact that I didn't notice until Thierry pointed it out to me. I decide to take a picture of it with my BlackBerry, and am galvanised by the sight.

The plan is to shave my patchy "chemo crop" exactly a month after my last chemotherapy treatment, and so, on 24 May, Thierry shaves his own head in my honour, and then uses his clippers to shave mine. Sitting in the bathroom at home, it is a more intimate Shavathon this time around, and all the more poignant because he missed the first one.

I find myself meticulously collecting every single hair that has dropped onto the floor and tossing it in the sink. When Thierry is finished shaving me, I gather all my hair into a ball (it's too little to call a handful) and, after a quick and cheeky goodbye, I flush it down the toilet.

In the shower afterwards, I feel the water running over my head, and I smile at the thought of how liberating it feels to get rid of that disliked hair on this particular day, a month since my last chemotherapy treatment. How far I have come, I think, on my journey through breast cancer – from the uncertainty of diagnosis to this very moment.

And it is on this same day, just a few hours after shaving my head, that I head to the Palazzo Montecasino Hotel for an interview and photo shoot with Media24, which follows a few weeks after an interview with Carte Blanche.

———◆———

I long ago disclosed my breast cancer diagnosis on social networks such as Facebook and BBM and Twitter, as I did with regards to my sobriety. But declining invitations from the media to speak about my diagnosis has been automatic – before now, and during the time of my chemotherapy treatments, it just didn't feel right to me to partake in media interviews. My interview with Carte Blanche is an epic shift for me, because I feel that my story may finally be of benefit to people who are doing battle with cancer, just as I have.

The end of my treatment has also coincided with Angelina Jolie's disclosure of her preventative mastectomy – shooting media interest in breast cancer to an all-time high.

When Dr Benn's rooms called to inform me of Carte Blanche's request for an interview with me, I knew that the invitation couldn't have come at a more appropriate time – I was now ready to give back.

———•———

The Carte Blanche interview takes place at the Palazzo Hotel shortly after my last chemo treatment. I arrive already dressed and prepped, and having done my make-up in the intervals between a number of hot flushes. Sitting on a couch in the main lounge of the penthouse just moments before the cameras start rolling, I intentionally remove my wig and wear my balding scalp with pride, with the big patch on the back of my head there for all to see. Here is my opportunity to share my journey and to let people know that cancer can happen to anyone. I hope that knowing about my cancer will help people who are still battling with theirs, and I hope that people who are in denial, as I was, might be inspired to take the necessary steps to save their own lives.

For me, the moment evokes huge emotion, and I feel it is life changing.

The interview goes well, and the feedback I receive after the show has been broadcast is extraordinary. I receive an outpouring of emails, texts, BBM and WhatsApp messages, posts on my Facebook page and enough calls, it feels, to fill an ocean.

My Twitter followers go from just over 200 to over 11 000 after the interview is aired.

———•———

A few weeks later, on the day of Thierry and my two-man Shavathon, I make my way to the car with my freshly shaven hair and a bag filled with jewellery, outfits and matching heels which I have been advised to bring along. Thierry, Zwelami and I are destined once again for the penthouse suite at the Palazzo Hotel, this time for the Media24 interview.

It's not too long before I'm sitting in my make-up chair, and then I'm ushered to the main bedroom.

I walk in very anxious, not knowing what to expect. After a conversational interview with the journalist, the photographer captures a few images of me, after which I am sent back to the second bedroom to select some of the outfits the stylist has spread out on the bed for me. My brother Zondwa has come along today too, leaving Zwelami entertaining himself on the computer in the penthouse's office. I call Zondwa and Thierry into the bedroom to assist me with finding the most flattering garments. My bag from home consists of casual clothing I have chosen that is not too "high end" or elegant, but the stylist prefers that I wear the clothes they have made available to me. I have completely forgotten that I would need to lose some weight before I can fit into certain sizes, but the guys help me with a few subtle head shakes and nods.

I put on a dress that the stylist has brought, and then I'm ready for the "official" photo shoot.

As the focus of attention for everyone in the entire penthouse, there I stand, positioned just a few feet from the balcony with its scenic view.

Then I'm back in the bedroom for a second change of outfits and a quick touch-up to my make-up. I chose a dress I really like, and which I would have worn from the beginning if the photographer hadn't chosen another one as his favourite. Back in the main bedroom, after the last pictures are taken of the second dress, the photographer asks to have a few shots of me in my wig, as all the other shots have been taken without one.

I have had no intention of wearing my wig in any of the pictures.

When the magazines are published a few weeks later, I am relieved to see that the pictures chosen for the *Huisgenoot* article, and both the *DRUM* and the *YOU* magazine covers are of me with my bald head.

———

Three days after the interview with Media24, I walk back into the Netcare Milpark Hospital, where I had my mastectomy – this time for an appointment with my plastic surgeon, Dr Slabbert. I haven't realised how long ago it's been since my last expansion treatment until he mentions that it was over nine months ago.

The first stage of breast reconstruction involves replacing breast tissue with tissue expanders. The second stage is then to replace the tissue expanders with a permanent prosthesis or implant. This is followed by nipple reconstruction, which is the third and final stage. After examining my breasts, Dr Slabbert says he feels it is now time to begin my second-stage breast reconstruction, and he begins to give us a rundown of what to expect for my first post-chemo surgery.

I have arrived for this appointment with the intention of deciding on implant sizes, only to be quickly corrected by Dr Slabbert, who informs me of how it is done: implants of different sizes are taken into theatre at the time of the surgery, and are then placed into the empty shell of your breasts once the tissue expanders have been removed in order to see which one produces the best fit. I implore him to take into consideration that, ideally, I want to have a slightly bigger implant to that of my current tissue expander size.

After the appointment ends, I have a few minutes with

the office manager of the practice, who gives me three dates to pick from for my breast reconstruction.

Naturally, I am anxious about my second-last surgery and I am extremely concerned that I may eventually have to live with a breast size that I am unhappy with. Exactly a week before the surgery, I decide to contact Dr Slabbert in an attempt to explain what is concerning me most: having a breast implant that is the same size as my tissue expanders. A few days after sending him the email, his office mails me back making a time to meet Dr Slabbert so he can address my worries and answer my many questions.

———

The next day, my grandfather is admitted back into hospital.

It is in the early hours of Saturday, 8 June 2013. My upcoming surgery suddenly pales in significance compared to my grandfather's medical condition and extended stay at the Pretoria hospital. In the greater scheme of things, what is more important is that I am there to support my grandfather.

One morning, on one of my daily visits to my ailing grandfather, I find myself calling Dr Slabbert's office to inform them that I am not in a position to undergo surgery at a time when my grandfather is so ill. For my own part, I cannot fathom lying in a hospital bed not knowing what news I might wake up to when I come round from the anaesthetic – it is simply not an option I am willing to avail myself to.

But days become weeks and concern becomes desperation.

Although I am seeing my grandfather almost every single day, I would much prefer to revert to our usual routine of twice-weekly visits, because then it would mean that he is home, and he is well. It brings me some comfort that I can travel to Pretoria so often to be with him, although I leave the hospital every day not knowing what his condition will be the next hour, let alone the next day.

But I always need to see for myself how he is doing.

Every day, by the time I get home from the hospital, I am so fagged that I can only just get myself to bed. The Tamoxifen leaves me with very little energy, despite the vitamin-B capsules I have added to my pill collection. I seriously need a boost these days, so as soon as Dr Demetriou gives me the green light, I find myself sitting on the bench outside the consulting room at the Fourways Mall Dis-Chem, awaiting a vitamin-B12 injection.

After loading my personal details onto her system, the nurse explains to me that some patients find the administration of the injection somewhat painful. Having just been through chemo, I think I can handle it. She asks me to expose my buttocks before sinking the needle into my skin and then applying a Band-Aid to the area. I'm rather taken aback by how the strong taste of the shot reaches my mouth just a second after she has injected me. I won't be doing that again.

Five days after my grandfather is hospitalised, a cousin of mine asks me whether I remember what my grandfather said to me after Zenani passed on. I recall quite clearly how, at my family home in Soweto, right in the room where Zenani, Zwelami and I used to sleep, my grandfather asked me to get up from the baseless mattress I was sitting on and come sit on his lap. I kept insisting that, at thirty years old, I was too grown up to do that, but he wouldn't have it.

Once I was sitting with him in the centre of the room, he said that many women would draw inspiration from me, and that what I had been subjected to with the loss of Zenani would strengthen me.

He said: "You are not the only one who has lost a child. I have lost a child and many people have, but for you it is so that you can bring hope to many."

It was a profound awakening for me, and I was completely overcome.

Bringing inspiration is a realisation of my dreams. From my family, I am drawing on a legacy that brings about change, and also one that instils hope.

—◦—

In the last few years, June has been a long and difficult month. It is the month of both Zenani and Zenawe's birthdays and also the anniversaries of their passing.

The month of June is always a depressing reminder of my unbearable loss.

June 2013 was made even more difficult with the experience of my grandfather's hospitalisation, and the impact that had on me, my family and the world at large.

But, in this most heartbreaking of months, life also turned out to be most beautiful.

At a time when my Aunt Zenani and I were fasting – each for our own reasons – I had my first menstrual cycle, bringing with it the renewal of all my hopes, both for my health and my future. When I saw it I jumped up from the toilet seat, screaming with absolute joy and triumph. My ovaries had kicked back on their own, and without any help, just over two months after my last chemotherapy treatment – I no longer had to await the return of my cycle.

"No wonder you were so moody the other day," Thierry smiled as he looked at me shining from the inside.

I couldn't wait to share the news with my loved ones, and I related the same story over and over again as I called my cousins, Thatohatsi and my grandmother, and sent a text to my Aunt Zenani, who immediately called me back from Buenos Aires.

In the same month, I signed a book deal, which provided yet another vehicle to drive breast cancer awareness. And just a few days later, I receive a call from Claude, informing me that an international station had shown interest in my documentary film.

As my grandfather said that day, I have found a most rewarding purpose. As I share the ebbs and flows of my life, I hope that people identify with me, find hope and, where necessary, a reason to change their life stories. And remember that despite the tragedies of life, there is always space for love, laughter and more hope.